OEDIPUS

by Sophocles

a version by Blake Morrison

ANTIGONE

by Sophocles

a version by Blake Morrison

NORTHERN BROADSIDES

First published 2003 by
Northern Broadsides, Dean Clough, Halifax HX3 5AX

ISBN: 0 9546422 0 1

Also by Blake Morrison

Dark Glasses
The Ballad of the Yorkshire Ripper
The Yellow House
And When Did You Last See Your Father?
As If
Too True
The Cracked Pot
Selected Poems
The Justification of Johann Gutenberg
Things My Mother Never Told Me

Designed and typeset by
Andi Chapple Design, Sedbergh, Cumbria
and printed by
The Cromwell Press, Trowbridge, Wiltshire

CONTENTS

Introduction by Blake Morrison

Classics escape the prison of time. Whichever their era, they belong to every other era. The classic doesn't have a sell-by date – if it did, it wouldn't be a classic.

The opening lines of *Oedipus* describe a plague afflicting Thebes, and in the spring of 2001 (when I began adapting the play for a modern stage-version) Britain was struggling with a plague of its own, the foot-and-mouth epidemic. Sophocles speaks of dying cattle and rotting meadows, and I knew that when the play toured in rural areas where pyres of sheep were commonplace (one of the venues was Skipton cattle market), there'd be huge resonance in those lines. But when the play had its press night two days after 9/11, the image of a ruined Thebes – reeking with smoke, ringing with cries, a panicked people massing in the squares – took on other meanings as well. Jocasta praying at a stone altar resembled the bewildered relatives at Ground Zero. Oedipus' promise to find the perpetrator and bring him to justice had the immediacy of a George Bush press conference. And Tiresias' tirade against Oedipus – when he tells him that his conspiracy-theories are foolish, and that the real culprit is himself – reminded me of the pundits who were saying that the US "had this coming".

Two years after that *Oedipus* production, I found myself working on *Antigone* against the background of war in Iraq. The enemy had been sent packing and a new regime was in place. But winning the peace was proving problematic: there were still pockets of resistance, and anxieties about how to deal with enemy corpses. In other words, the struggle between Creon and Antigone was still going on 2,500 years after Sophocles wrote his play.

Northern Broadsides like to take the classics into communities and parts of the country which theatre doesn't always reach. That sense of mission has left its mark on these two texts. Zeus and Dionysus are present but so are the landscapes of the

Barrie Rutter (left) and Blake Morrison. Photo: Giuseppe Belli

Yorkshire Dales; and through the lines of blank verse, and the lyrics of the Chorus, there's the music of a rough-tongued northern vernacular. Occasionally I depart from Sophocles (in beginning *Antigone* with the choric victory celebrations, for instance), because the performance seemed to demand it. But I've tried to honour the spirit of the original, in a language really spoken by men.

Marx believed that Ancient Greek culture shows us the "childhood of man". But that's to confuse simplicity with naivety and directness with lack of sophistication. *Oedipus* may be a primal myth, but it also has the intricacy of a detective mystery. And the central debate of *Antigone* – family versus state – is as burning an issue in the twenty-first century as it was in 445BC.

Rutter writes ...

No wonder I like the Classics – the Greeks, Shakespeare – and the classical form of language, big lines, big ideas: language to rock and roll by, rhythms to carry in the holy trinity of head, heart and guts; assonance, alliteration, iambics, rhetoric needing big breaths, powerful lungs, lingual stamina, labial stamina, memory stamina – it's Food! Great, gorgeous, steaming tureens of food: and it tastes wonderful. The tactile sensuality of bringing to life the in-built performability that the ancient poets crammed their texts with is one of the great pleasures of theatrical life: the relish of wrapping my gob around and over consonants, clanging and clashing the short vowels, revelling in the pulse, surfboarding with the verse. Verse calls attention to itself: "Look at me," it says, "listen to me." Yeats said of his rendition of 'Lake Isle of Innisfree',

"I wrote it as verse, I'll be damned if I'm going to make it sound like prose."
Well said, WB.

I too will be damned if I ever succumb to the slaughter of the verse form, the chopping up of it like sliced sausages, the delivery of it reminiscent of a stuttering carburettor, the underlining of pronouns, adverbs and adjectives that is so prevalent today – chop logic, chop English, about as much interest and passion as chop suey. "What's this mean, Rutter?" My reply – "It's a rhyming couplet, hit the form and it'll tell you what it means." Simple! Not as simple as it should be but the battle gets easier within Northern Broadsides as the plays roll by.

Our authors of Shakespeare, Sophocles/Morrison, Kleist/Morrison, Harrison, Hughes, Milton are a pantheon of poetry – revellers of words.

The obituary of the legendary Greek actor Alexis Minotis in 1990 contained this from the actor: "Always remember that Greek tragedy is about 'the word'; it requires rhythm, meaningful and heightened delivery, for it is the loftiest manifestation of the human spirit."

Translation adds a certain exaggeration, but by Hell, I know what he's talking about.

Rutter

OEDIPUS

by Sophocles
a version by Blake Morrison, 2001

CHARACTERS

OEDIPUS

JOCASTA, his wife

CREON, his brother-in-law

TIRESIAS, a prophet

SPOKESMAN

MESSENGER

SHEPHERD

SERVANT

CHORUS

ANTIGONE/ISMENE (silent)

Oedipus was first performed at The Viaduct Theatre, Dean Clough, Halifax on 6th September 2001 with the following Northern Broadsides cast:

Chorus/Spokesman	Andrew Vincent
Chorus/Messenger	Dawson Peters
Chorus/Shepherd	Dennis Conlon
Chorus/Servant	Christine Cox
Chorus	Andy Wear
Chorus	Andrew Whitehead
Chorus	Michelle Hardwick
Oedipus	Conrad Nelson
Creon	John Branwell
Tiresias	Barrie Rutter
Jocasta	Sarah Parks
Director	Barrie Rutter
Designer	Jessica Worrall
Composer	Conrad Nelson

Scene: in front of Oedipus' house. A crowd of citizens, weak and destitute; a mood of anger and despair. Enter OEDIPUS, limping – he's concerned yet arrogant, charismatic but a touch too full of himself.

OEDIPUS
Now then – what brings you milling round my gates?
Aren't there groans enough in town already
without your wailing? Haven't you homes to go to,
rather than camping out? "Oedipus," they said,
"there's a problem, people are on the streets."
I could have sent a deputy to deal with it,
but you know me. Out with it, then: what brings you?
something you want? or something you're afraid of?
You can tell me: I'm not made of marble.
And even marble would melt hearing your lamb-bleats
and seeing you mewed together at my feet.

SPOKESMAN
You can see what a mixed bag we are –
young lads with no future, brides learning how
to be widows, farmers with nowt to farm.
What's happening here is happening all over –
there are folks like us on every corner,
the clam of death on them and all with one question:
where's the man who can save us from this mess?
  The place is falling apart, waste and rubble
everywhere you look. Nothing works
and no one visits. Barren harvests,
cows with their ribs showing like roof-slats,
vast pyres of mouldering sheep – that's the meadows.
Here in town we've got it as bad or worse.
Fever trickles in beads down lime-white cheeks.
Babies whine for their mums and mums keen o'er
their babies. The plague's left its mark on every door.
  It's not because we reckon you're a god
that we've fetched up at your doorstep
but because we rate you first among men.
Before you limped here out of nowhere
all those years back, the Sphinx had us by the throat.
She'd set a puzzle no one could answer:
"Which creature goes on four legs in the morning,
two in the afternoon, and three at night?"
Our finest minds were foxed. Then you came.
We couldn't tell you how to fix the bitch,
but with the gods on your side you cracked it.
"Man," you answered, "who crawls when he's a baby,

walks upright as an adult, and in old age
uses a stick." Plain as duck-eggs once you've heard it,
but brilliant all the same. By solving that riddle,
you lifted the Sphinx's curse.
That's why you're our hero,
Oedipus, that's why we're here on hands and knees
begging you to rid us of this disease.
You're in with the gods – can't they tell you what to do?
Or can't you draw on what life has learned you?
You rescued us once before; well, do it again.
You made us promises; don't go back on them.
The man who saved us when we were lost at sea
and then let us drown in the shallows –
is that how you want to be remembered?
No, a town without townsfolk is a ghost ship.
And a captain isn't worthy of the name
if his crew's dead and his boat sinking from shame.

OEDIPUS

If I say nothing, don't take my silence amiss.
It's not that I'm short of feeling; I feel
for you all too much. You're sick, but I'm sicker.
The pain you suffer is yours alone; the pain
I feel is that of everyone in my keeping,
you and you and you. You didn't wake me
by coming here, I've been up pacing all night
like a doctor sifting his books for a cure.
And the one sure remedy I came up with
I've acted on, sending my brother-in-law,
Creon, to consult the oracle.
He's been gone ages now – a sight more hours
than a trek that distance should have taken him.
But when he comes he'll bring a message too –
and whatever the gods demand of me I'll do.

SPOKESMAN

Funny you should say that – he's just been spotted.

OEDIPUS

Let's hope he has good news.

SPOKESMAN

It must be good.
He looks like he's dressed up for a party.

enter CREON

OEDIPUS
Creon, friend and brother, what's the message?

CREON
"When a day fairs up cobbled roads turn smooth
and cartloads feel faffly as a feather."

OEDIPUS
I can't tell whether to grieve or celebrate.
The message, Creon – what did the oracle say?

CREON
Do I have to tell you in front of them?
Come on, let's have a quiet word inside.

OEDIPUS
Say it right out. There are no secrets with us.
The health of these people means more to me
than even my own.

CREON
Here's what was said, then.
That to banish the plague, we've to destroy
the source of infection. We're stuck until we do.

OEDIPUS
Yes? But what source? and how? It's very vague.

CREON
The source of the infection is a man –
a murderer. Exile him, or shed his blood
in retribution, then we'll be cured.
It's from him that all our troubles have sprung.

OEDIPUS
So who's the man causing the problem?

CREON
It's a long story. It goes back to when
Laius was in charge here, before your time.

OEDIPUS
As you know, I never met Laius –
sad to say, he's only a name to me.

CREON
Laius was murdered. And the gods say
whoever murdered him must be made to pay.

OEDIPUS
But how can we find them when they've long since fled
the scene and the corpse is nothing but a worm-bag?

CREON
They're here, so I was told. Seek, and live in hope.
Don't bother seeking, and we're all dead rope.

OEDIPUS
So where was it that Laius met his doom?
At home? Somewhere in the country? Abroad?

CREON
He'd gone on a little trip, a pilgrimage.
We know he set out, but he never came back.

OEDIPUS
But there must have been witnesses. Wasn't someone
travelling with him, whose evidence could help?

CREON
They were all killed, but for one man who scarpered.
And his memory of it was useless
– he'd wiped the lot, except for one thing.

OEDIPUS
What was that, then? The tiniest clue,
even from him, might be a breakthrough.

CREON
The killers were a bunch of thugs, he said –
outlaws, muggers, scum from over the border –
not a lone robber, but a great gang of them.

OEDIPUS
But Laius was a leader, a man of substance.
How would a stranger – or strangers – have had the nerve?
Unless someone he knew had it in for him
and hired some hard-up lads to do the deed ...

CREON
That was one theory. But with Laius dead,
we were all at sea, and there was no captain
to steer the way forward.

OEDIPUS

But the way forward
was obvious: Laius has been murdered,

so your job's to find out who did it.

CREON
We would have, but then the Sphinx confused us
with her riddle and we missed what was under our nose.

OEDIPUS
Right, I'll start from scratch and bring these things to light.
It's the least I can do – and I'm doing it
not for some relation I never met,
but to cleanse a wound that still infects us.
For myself, too: whoever killed Laius
could one day turn his bloody hand against me,
so in bringing his killer to justice
I'm also looking after number one.
  Off, then, gather your things, spread the word
throughout the town till everyone's heard.
My mission's to bring the killer to the dock.
If I don't, it'll be my head on the block.

exit OEDIPUS and CREON

SPOKESMAN
We've got what we came for: let's be on us way.
No future in hanging round ...

exit SPOKESMAN and some of CHORUS – but others stay, or enter

CHORUS
                                        ... Now let us pray:
Zeus, immortal leader, god of gods,
whose feet we are not fit to lick, to whom
we bow our heads and bend our knocking knees,
fearing what holy terrors you've in store,
I beg you ...
                ... Apollo, I beg you,
if ever you've harnessed the sun to plough up
the storm-fields of disaster or drive off
the clouds of misery from man's gates,
do it again, please, now ...
                                    ... Please, Athena,
loveliest daughter, brainchild of Zeus' head,
make our lives sweet as a milkchurn again,
hear us when we call ...
                                ... hear us when we call,
Artemis, wise protectress of our crops,

enemy of the rancid cow-tick
and twiny sheep-louse. We humbly ask you ...
... ask you,
Apollo, to deliver us from our suffering
and mop the fever from our clammy brow.

Nothing escapes the plague – it's invaded
every last pore. Grapes wither on the vine.
The wheat's too waufish to grow an ear.
Women in labour haven't the bauf
to push their babies out ...
... Little lives sink in the west
each dusk, like birds flocking after the sun,
till only one bird's left – the black raven
of death, flapping its wings in our faces
and raking our eyes out with its claws ...
... The corpse-carts have buckled from overloading.
The dead lie stinking on open ground.
Roupy children wind to school in a cortege.
Young wives made grey by weeping join hands
with their white-haired mothers at the altar.
Please answer their call, Artemis ... hear them,
Athena, it's your kind face they're looking at.
Send disease packing ...
... strike it stone-dead, Zeus,
blow it away with gales, raze it with stormclaps,
crush it with thunder, let blizzards cool its fever
and rain-swollen rivers wash it clean. ...
... And shine your lightning in every corner, Zeus,
in case it's hiding ...
... shame it out with arrows
of fire, Apollo ... hunt it with torches, Artemis ...
... and you, Dionysus, supper host, music god,
master of ceremonies, king of satyrs,
whose praises we once sung as we supped wine,
bring heat and laughter back into our hearts ...
... till the skulking plague god – the god hated
by all other gods – dies in a blaze of light.

enter OEDIPUS

OEDIPUS

I can't believe it, they're on their knees again.
They need to be told. *[addresses them]* Get up, will you,
and listen to reason. He's your god here.
Listen to reason and your troubles will pass.

I came to this town as an outsider,
knowing nothing of my predecessor
or of when, where, why and how he was killed.
But I'm a resident now, I've lived here years,
my children grew up here, I speak the same tongue
as you do, if we put our heads together
we can crack the case. So here are my orders.
If anybody knows who murdered Laius,
they must tell me and swear it under oath.
Don't be afraid of implicating yourself.
Even if you're the one who murdered him,
I promise you'll leave alive and unharmed –
your punishment will be exile, that's all.
On the other hand, if it was a stranger
who did it – a traveller, a thug, some scum-face
from over the border, a foreigner scuttling in
by the back door and taking what by rights
should have been yours – then if you know who he is
give me his name and I'll have it sorted out.
But if you clam up and shrink from confessing
and won't grass on your best friend or next of kin,
then whoever you are you're a traitor.
As the oracle said, this man's dangerous.
None of you must take him in, give him food
or pass the time of day with him; every door
must be bolted fast against his infection.
I make these orders in honour of the gods
and out of respect for the victim.
Two more things. One, whether this man acted alone
or in a gang, he must be made to grasp
what evil means. Two, if ever *I* shake his hand
or give him houseroom, I ask to be dealt with
as roughly as any of you would be –
yes, send me away for breaking my own laws.
Those are my orders. Make sure they're obeyed.
For even if the oracle hadn't told us
to do this, it wouldn't be right to let it rest –
when a leader is scrubbed away like dirt,
when a man in his prime comes home as a corpse,
we've a duty to establish what went on.
Now I hold the reins that Laius once held,
and sleep in his bed, and the mother of my children
is the same woman who used to be his wife
(which binds me and Laius even tighter
since he, given more time and better luck,
was planning to have children with her too),

for all those reasons I'll see this case through
as though the man who died were my own father.
I'll go to the wall finding his killer –
this I promise, strike me stone-blind if I don't.
And if any man defies my orders,
let all the seeds he's planted in the soil
or in his wife perish and shrivel to nothing –
while you good people who stick to my law
prosper and multiply for evermore.

CHORUS

You've laid it out and given solemn orders,
so you can take it I'm speaking under oath.
I didn't kill Laius, nor do I know who did.
But I can't help wondering why the message
the gods sent didn't make it easier for us.
Since they know who did it, why won't they say?

OEDIPUS

Fair point. But you know what the gods are like:
if they're not in the mood to do a thing
no power on earth can force them – it's their nature.

CHORUS

Right enough – but I've a second point.

OEDIPUS

Why not make a third while you're at it?

CHORUS

If we're looking where to find an answer,
the best bet after the gods is Tiresias –
he knows all there is to know, and more.

OEDIPUS

Do you suppose I haven't thought of that?
Twice I've asked Creon to have him fetched.
It's a mystery why he's not here already.

CHORUS

He's your last hope. All the other rumours
are woolly as sheep.

OEDIPUS

Which rumours are those?

CHORUS

It's said Laius was murdered by gypsies.

OEDIPUS
Yes, I've heard that one. But the man who started it –
nobody's seen him in years.

CHORUS
                                        Maybe not.
But once he gets wind of your orders,
he'll be straight round, won't he? Or else the killer
will be so terrified he'll confess.

OEDIPUS
I doubt it. A man who's not afraid
to murder won't get the wind up at mere words.

CHORUS
But someone might catch him out – and here's
the likeliest, the prophet Tiresias.
If any man's in touch with the truth, it's him.

enter TIRESIAS

OEDIPUS
Tiresias, our town's greatest living prophet,
whose footsoles tread the same earth as we do
but whose head dwells up there in the stars,
who may be blind but can see clear as daylight
what the plague's done – you're our only hope, old son,
we look to you to save us from disaster.
  No doubt you've heard that when we asked the gods
what we should do to be shot of our sorrows,
their answer was "Find the men who killed Laius,
and execute them or send them in exile".
Now since the gods have been so obliging,
I trust you will be too. Whatever powers you have,
magic spells, card tricks, voices in your head,
tea leaves, rooks' feathers, witches' brews, cloud shapes,
the wisdom of owls or overance of eagles –
whatever your method, use it, and save me,
save yourself, save all of us from the curse
of Laius' murder. We're in your hands.
Here's a chance to demonstrate your talents.
Was ever the gift of vision better employed?

TIRESIAS
A fat lot of good vision has done me.
If I'd had vision when you asked me here
I'd have thought twice about it and not come.

OEDIPUS
Stop blethering. What are you on about?

TIRESIAS
Let me go home – that's what I'm asking.
Things'll turn out better for us both if you do.

OEDIPUS
Let you go home? But you've only just got here.
You're given the chance to save your own town
and you spurn it, you glumpy old sod? I'm dumbstruck.

TIRESIAS
Well, I'm dumbstruck too. Better saying nowt
than letting anger like yours spew out.

OEDIPUS
I invited you here, in all courtesy,
to do us a favour. So get a move on –
we're not letting you leave till you deliver.

TIRESIAS
You want me to speak because you don't know the truth.
I do know – that's why I'll never reveal it.
My griefs are best left unsaid – aye, and *yours*, too.

OEDIPUS
Have I got this right? You know the truth
but rather than say it out loud you'd let
your own people die from the plague? Is that it?

TIRESIAS
I won't inflict pain on myself or others.
That's all there is to it. I've said enough.

OEDIPUS
You're harder than a rockface. More stubborn too.
Even a boulder could lose its temper with you.

TIRESIAS
Your temper's your own lookout. Did I provoke it?

OEDIPUS
You did, yes – to hear our town being treated
with such contempt, who wouldn't lose his rag?

TIRESIAS
The future will happen, whether I tell it you

or not.

OEDIPUS

You might as well tell it me, then.

TIRESIAS

That's it, I've spoken my last word. Fill the air
by ranting at me all you like, I don't care.

OEDIPUS

Too true I'll rant, and I'll do more. I'll add up
the sum of what you said, I'll put two and two
together and make four. As I see it,
you must have been in on the plot against Laius –
yes, dreamt it up and carried out the whole thing,
short of killing him with your own hands;
and if you weren't blind, you'd have done that too.

TIRESIAS

Is that so? In that case, I'm quoting your own law
back at you: from now on you're forbidden
to have contact with any of us.
The source of this town's infection is *you*.

OEDIPUS

Which pothole of your brain spouted that one?
I've heard of guilty men shifting the blame
onto others with some trick or alibi,
but you're shameless. If you think you'll escape
with your life, forget it.

TIRESIAS

I will escape,
that's certain – I know the future, you see.

OEDIPUS

Who put you up to this?

TIRESIAS

You did. Remember?
You made me speak when I didn't want to.

OEDIPUS

Speak again, then. Spit it out. Let's be sure
we heard you correctly.

TIRESIAS

You heard all right.

Don't make me go over it.

OEDIPUS

But you must,
we might have misheard you.

TIRESIAS

In plain words, then:
You killed the man whose killer you're looking for.

OEDIPUS

Twice now you've said it. You'll die for this.

TIRESIAS

Shall I add something else from my death-cell?

OEDIPUS

Whatever you like – it's all lies any road.

TIRESIAS

I'll tell you then. You're polluted, you stink –
you've been biding in sin with your own kin.

OEDIPUS

Go on, scatter your fancies. You're like a farmer
sowing grass-seed in a winter gale.

TIRESIAS

It's only the truth, Oedipus. There's strength in truth.

OEDIPUS

There is, but there's none in you. You're mad.
You're more cracked than a pot dropped on flagstones.

TIRESIAS

I pity you for having to hound me like this.
Soon everyone in town'll be hounding you.

OEDIPUS

Really? No one's set their dogs on me yet.
And when they do, I'll drive them off with torches.
I live in the light – I've nothing to fear
from a lump of darkness like you.

TIRESIAS

That's true,
as it happens – it's not me who'll destroy you,
the gods have already decided that.

OEDIPUS
Creon! Of course! You're not in this alone.

TIRESIAS
Creon's not your enemy. You are your own.

OEDIPUS
Whenever power joins with wisdom and wealth,
there's always jealousy as well, sidling up
with his green eyes and poisonous tongue.
I never sought power, the town gave it me for free –
but Creon, whom I trusted as a brother,
envied my position, and started keeking at every keyhole,
and dreamt up schemes to force me from office,
and hired himself this fairground huckster,
this hack, this cardsharp, this sexless Cassandra,
whose only eye is for profit not prophecy,
and who can see no better than a castrated ram
lost on the hilltops in a heavy fog.
  Come on, Mr T, the great clairvoyant,
let's make a cool appraisal of your talents.
When the Sphinx set her riddle, where were you?
The town was desperate, it cried out for
a man of vision, but you – with your leprechauns
and bird voices – you failed the test, you were stumped,
all your years of training came to nothing.
Then I arrived, a stranger, a passer-by,
a man with few gifts and no apprenticeship
limping out of nowhere on a gammy leg,
know-nothing Oedipus, and I beat that bitch,
I cracked her riddle quicker than you can blink,
and I didn't use birds or magic mushrooms –
I found the answer through my own wits.
  The better man taking over your patch –
it's no wonder you wanted me out of the road.
But if you thought clubbing up with Creon
was any way to see me off you're dafter than I thought.
I'm tempted to fetch a whip to teach you
loyalty, or to clatter you about the head
until you truly see stars. But you're such
a mardy old eunuch I can't be fussed.

CHORUS
In our view, you're both wrong. Anger's burning
your hearts when you should be using your heads.
Your job's to beat the plague, as the oracle said.

TIRESIAS

Throw your weight around all you like, big man,
but I'm your equal, and I'll have my say.
The gods are the only masters I obey –
I don't take orders from the likes of Creon, or you.
Go on, mock me like some taunting schoolkid
and chuck my blindness back in my face,
but if you can't you see the sty you're living in –
and who you share it with – your eyes are worse than mine.
Do you know even who your parents are? Nah. You're blind,
deaf, dumb, stone-dead in every one of your senses,
and in your ignorance you've done dirt
on your closest relations, both living and dead.
You fancy yourself now, but soon your mother's curse,
aye and your father's, will fetch you a double blow,
like a pair of fingers jabbed in the eyeballs,
and then you'll know what darkness looks like.
  And when you cry out in pain, no one will come.
You'll be a hermit on a far black hill.
Every rockface will echo with your groans.
And the marriage you thought a feathery bed
will be shown for the jagged outcrop it is,
a stony moortop of bramble and gorse.
  And that's only the start. Wherever you look – in the mirror,
in the past, in your children's faces –
a thousand more horrors are lying in wait,
your worst nightmares are about to come true.
Crap on Creon, make a mockery of me,
no man has ever been crushed as you'll be.

OEDIPUS

Enough! Out of my sight and don't come back.

TIRESIAS

I'd no wish to come; I only did as asked.

OEDIPUS

How was I to know what rubbish he'd talk?
He'd never have been invited if I'd guessed.

TIRESIAS

Do you call it rubbish? I doubt your parents –
your *real* parents – would call it that.

OEDIPUS

You what?
Tell me, wise prophet: who is my father, then?

TIRESIAS
You don't know you're born, do you. But you will be born,
today – and your birth'll be the death of you.

OEDIPUS
Stop talking in riddles. Your tongue's as sleek
as a wet eel-skin. Speak plainly for once.

TIRESIAS
I thought solving riddles was a gift of yours.

OEDIPUS
That's it, ridicule the thing I'm famous for.

TIRESIAS
You thought it was a mark of greatness, didn't you?
But that was the moment your troubles began.

OEDIPUS
How can you say that? I saved the people.

TIRESIAS
Saved? Destroyed! They're dropping like rotten fruit.
If you can't see that, it's pointless me talking.
I'm off.

OEDIPUS
Suits me, I've things to do, get walking.

TIRESIAS
Don't worry, Action Man, I'm on my way,
but first there's one last thing I have to say.
I'm not afraid of your threats – I've seen the ending
and I know you can't hurt me. So listen:
The man you're looking for, Laius' killer,
lives right here in Thebes. He thinks he's a foreigner,
but he's about to discover he's a native.
And when he does, he won't be best pleased,
because this will follow: he'll lose his precious sight,
he'll become a beggar instead of a rich man,
and he'll be driven out of town in shame,
a white stick tip-tapping the way ahead.
There's a load more he'll discover too:
that he's brother and father to his children,
that he's son and husband to his mother,
that he's heir and killer of his dad.
So use your wits and riddle that one out.

And if I'm proved wrong, next time I won't mind
you mocking my prophecies and calling me blind.

exit TIRESIAS and OEDIPUS

CHORUS
Who is it with blood on his hands?
Whose sin was it brought the plague?
Whoever the man,
he'll have to gallop
faster than a stallion,
he'll have to fly
like a leaf in a hurricane,
he'll have to streak
like lightning,
if he wants to escape –
the furies are closing
for the kill.

From the dankest valley
to the iciest fell,
word's out to hunt him down.
Whether he's creeping
like a marten through a pine forest,
or skulking like a bull
in a moorland shippon,
his time's running out.
He can shut his eyes
to what's happening,
but the nets are
tightening – the gods
will get him in the end.

That was a strange riddle
Tiresias came out with.
I don't know if it's true.
But I can't disprove it, either.
I'm at a loss – all I know is
it worries me, deeply worries me.
I've no gift of foresight,
I can barely see
what's under my nose,
but in the pit of my heart I know
something bad's going to happen.
There's nothing in the past,

no sin or family feud,
that would justify me
thinking badly of Oedipus –
yet I've this sense of doom.

The gods know everything,
but how a mortal can claim
to know the future
any more than I do –
that baffles me.
Aye, people have talents,
and some are wiser than others,
but until we have proof
why believe these accusations
against our leader?
We know he had the brains
to outwit the Sphinx,
that was his great test
and he passed it.
He's a hero, we're all in his debt.
No, it *can't* be true –
I refuse to believe he's guilty.

enter CREON

CREON
What's this about Oedipus accusing me?
I'm his brother-in-law. How dare he!
I've done him no harm and yet he lays
all our troubles at my door. How can he say
I'm a traitor, me? I'd rather be dead
than have that branded on my forehead.
To know that everyone, even friends like you,
is suspicious of me ...

CHORUS
It wasn't thought through.
He said it in anger. He'll soon see the light.

CREON
But everyone heard him. Am I not right?
That it was me who egged on Tiresias?

CHORUS
It's true, that's what he thinks, though how he's
got there we don't know.

CREON

Was he calm when he spoke,
was his gaze level? did his voice choke?

CHORUS

Hard to tell – you can't fathom such men.
Anyway, here he is coming back again.

enter OEDIPUS

OEDIPUS

I'm stunned, Creon – you dare to show your face
after plotting to kill me and take over?
Tell me, what made you think you could succeed?
Did you take me for weak or merely stupid?
Was I meant not to see you carrying the knife?
Or see it but not put up a fight?
Well, it's you who's weak and stupid. Oust me?
You and whose army?

CREON

All right, have your laugh,
but before you start accusing people
let's get the facts straight.

OEDIPUS

Oh, I'm sure you'll be foxy
with the facts. You're dainty as an otter
with a salmon in its maw.

CREON

Can I just say something. ...

OEDIPUS

That you're *not* a traitor? Don't waste your breath.

CREON

If you're too much of a hothead to listen,
you're past help, your brain's smitten with fever.

OEDIPUS

So's yours if you think you can conspire against me –
against your own family – and not be punished.

CREON

What is it I'm reckoned to have done, then?

OEDIPUS

Did you or did you not advise me

to consult that cranky old prophet?

CREON

I did.

And I'd happily advise you to again.

OEDIPUS

And how many years is it since Laius ... ?

CREON

Since Laius did what? What are you getting at?

OEDIPUS

Since he disappeared. Since he was murdered.

CREON

I don't know, you'd have to go back a fair while.

OEDIPUS

And at that time, was Tiresias already around?

CREON

He was, he's been around for ever,
folks swear by him.

OEDIPUS

And did he mention my name then?

CREON

Not that I know of. Not in my company.

OEDIPUS

But didn't you rack your brains about the murder?
Didn't you ask yourself who the guilty man was?

CREON

We did, of course. But we got nowhere.

OEDIPUS

So how was it Tiresias didn't produce
these allegations back then? Tell me that.

CREON

I can't tell you. I don't pretend to know.

OEDIPUS

But you know one thing, don't you?

CREON

What's that, then?

OEDIPUS
You know that if you'd not spoken to him,
he'd not have said it was me who killed Laius.

CREON
I suppose that's true. If that's what he *did* say –
I wasn't there to hear him, remember.
Anyway, I've got some questions for you.

OEDIPUS
Fire away. You'll not hang the murder on me.

CREON
Well, then: it's true my sister is your wife?

OEDIPUS
No argument there. You know she is.

CREON
And you and she have equal powers in this town?

OEDIPUS
We do. Anything she wants, I give it her.

CREON
And isn't it also true that I own
a third share – that I'm treated as your equal?

OEDIPUS
Aye, and that's what makes your treachery worse.

CREON
It would do. But think carefully about this,
apply some logic for once. If a man can choose,
does he want the sweat and fear that go with power?
or is he happier sleeping at night?
I've no desire to be gaffer round here;
I have all I need already – why bother,
just for the sake of a fancier title?
Any man in his right mind would say the same.
As things stand, I get whatever I ask for;
if I had your job, it'd be a headache,
I'd be lugging duties round like a heavy sack.
  Power without responsibility – who can beat it?
To stroll the corridors like a titan
without enduring the cares of office:
I'd be a fool to chuck it away.
When I go out and about, people nod and smile,

they look up to me, I'm respected,
it's known if someone wants to bend *your* ear,
their best bet's have a word with Creon first.
Who in that position would turn traitor?
What's in it for me, high as I am, to go higher?
Which state's more perfect than the *status quo*?
If you don't believe me, check with the oracle
to see that I delivered the message right.
And if you discover I've been in a plot
with Tiresias, then have me killed on the spot –
it'd be the right sentence, I grant you.
But unless you've proof, so long as you're led
only by whim, then you've no right to accuse me.
To call good men bad is as dangerous
as taking bad men to be good. And to lose
a trusted friend is as daft as topping yourself
or chucking out your one good pair of shoes.

CHORUS
That's well said. If you've any sense, you'll listen,
Oedipus. Only fools charge in.

OEDIPUS
No, with traitors
you have to move fast. Dither and dawdle,
and they'll have a blindfold on before you blink.
Turn your back, and they'll plant a knife in it.
My best defence is to get in first.

CREON
And do what? Banish me?

OEDIPUS
No. I want your head
lopped off and paraded round town on a pole.

CREON
So you'll not even give me a fair hearing?

OEDIPUS
I've heard enough. Why listen to more?

CREON
Because you're not in your right mind.

OEDIPUS
I've a mind
for what's in my interests.

CREON

What about my interests?

OEDIPUS

As far as I can make out, what interests you
is laying plots against me.

CREON

What if you're wrong?

OEDIPUS

I can't afford to be – I'm leader round here.

CREON

Call this leadership!

OEDIPUS

Hark at him, people.

CREON

They're my people as well. I belong here as much as you.

CHORUS

Stop it, will you. You're like a pair of cockerels
scrapping in a ring. Here comes Jocasta –
just in time. Maybe she can knock some sense in you.

enter JOCASTA

JOCASTA

What a family! Aren't you ashamed to make
such a din when this town's sick and grieving?
Come inside, Oedipus; Creon, go home.
We've enough on without you beldering like this.

CREON

It's your husband who's to blame for it.
He intends to execute me – or send me
into exile. Go ahead and ask him.

OEDIPUS

He's a traitor. I caught him in an outhouse
sharpening his axe to assassinate me.

CREON

Don't listen – not a word of it is true.

JOCASTA

What's wrong with you, Oedipus? He's my brother.

Believe him. Have some sense. What will people say?

CHORUS
We say she's right, Oedipus. Your head's hot
and you're flying round in circles – just slow down.

OEDIPUS
You expect me to hang there, limp as a bat,
pretending not to see what's going on?

CHORUS
We expect you to remember who Creon is –
one of your family, a man you once trusted.

OEDIPUS
And so I've to ignore his treachery?

CHORUS
We didn't say that.

OEDIPUS
                    Then what did you say?

CHORUS
That it's wrong to start accusing someone
when your evidence is whiffly as an oak leaf –
least of all a man who's kith and kin.

OEDIPUS
Then I was right. You're asking me to fix up
my own downfall.

CHORUS
                    No! All we're asking
is that you find an easement for the plague,
not waste your breath on false accusations.

OEDIPUS
All right, then, let him go. If the price I pay
is my ruin, don't say I didn't warn you.
It's out of love for you I'm doing this,
remember. For him I feel only hate.

CREON
You're as surly in letting me go
as you were rash in charging me first off.
It can't be easy for a man to live with himself,
when his head's like a boar's roasting on a spit.

OEDIPUS
I know I should have topped you. Now get out.

CREON
I'm off, why stay here to be abused?
Everyone knows I'm innocent but you.

exit CREON

CHORUS *[to JOCASTA, referring to OEDIPUS]*
He's worse than a bull when it's seen red.
Best take him inside and cool his head.

JOCASTA
I will, once I get to the bottom of this.
How did it start?

CHORUS
From suspicion on one side
and hurt pride on the other. It were just words.

JOCASTA
So they were both as bad as each other.

CHORUS
Yes.

JOCASTA
And what was it exactly they said?

CHORUS
Don't go worrying yourself about that ...
We've troubles enough ... Let sleeping dogs lie.

OEDIPUS *[to CHORUS]*
All this coddling and in-betweening of yours –
it makes me sick. You leant on me to go easy
on my enemy; now he's roaming the streets.

CHORUS
We'd be stupid to stick up for Creon
if it were risky. We're on your side ...
No man's a truer friend of the people ...
You rescued us from the Sphinx ... You've seen us
on our knees at your gates ... It's why we came,
because we want you to save us again.

CHORUS withdraw

JOCASTA
I don't get it, either. What's mithering you?

OEDIPUS
I don't mind telling *you*, Jocasta – you're my wife,
I can trust you. Creon has been plotting
against me.

JOCASTA
Let's have the proof. How did it start?

OEDIPUS
With him saying it was me who killed Laius.

JOCASTA
Was that because he knows it for a fact?
Or did he hear a rumour from someone?

OEDIPUS
Oh, he took care not to plump me with it
straight to my face. He'd not have the gall.
Tiresias was sent to do his dirty work.

JOCASTA
Tiresias! Then you can stop worrying.
He's only a prophet and there's no prophet
on earth worth listening to. I found this out
the hard way, years ago, when a message
came to Laius – not direct from the gods, mind,
but through one of these Tiresias sorts –
saying if ever we had a son together
that son was set to take his father's life.
How true a prediction was it, then?
How bound by the gods were we? I'll tell you.
Laius, so everyone says, was killed
by a gang of foreigners – thugs, gypsies,
bandits, hoodlums – at a place where three roads meet;
and the son we had was less than three days old
when Laius, to be safe, had him taken away,
his feet bound together at the ankles,
to be left to die in the trackless wilds.
So much for prophecies, eh? The son I bore
barely lived long enough to suck my breast,
let alone kill his father; and Laius
was murdered by a bunch of foreigners,
a terrible fate, but not the death he feared.
That's why I've no time for the Tiresiases

of this world. Pay him no attention.
When the gods have a ticket with your number on
they deliver it in person.

OEDIPUS

I see that.
But something you just said scares me rigid.

JOCASTA
What do you mean? I said nothing to worry you.

OEDIPUS
I thought I heard you say Laius was killed
where three roads meet.

JOCASTA

That was the story.

OEDIPUS
How long ago was this?

JOCASTA

Before your time –
but only just. You arrived shortly after.

OEDIPUS
What else have you gods in store for me?

JOCASTA
What's wrong?

OEDIPUS

Don't ask. Tell me about Laius:
what did he look like, tall, short, young, old,
thin as a rake or had he a fleece on him?

JOCASTA
He was tall. Dark-haired but with a cauf-lick
of grey at the front, like a badger's stripe.
And his build – well, not so different from yours.

OEDIPUS
Then I'm doomed. The executioner
won't have far to look. It's my head on the anvil.
I can see his blade flashing in the sun.

JOCASTA
Don't maunder like this. You're frightening me.

OEDIPUS
It seems Tiresias has eyes after all.
One more question and then I'll know for sure.

JOCASTA
I'm afraid to answer, but go on, ask me.

OEDIPUS
Was Laius travelling in a small party?
Or, being leader, had he a heavy escort?

JOCASTA
There were five of them, that's all, including a boy
who ran messages. And just the one carriage,
which only Laius was allowed to ride in.

OEDIPUS
It's clear as a valley bottom after the dawn mist
has burned off. And who reported it?
There must have been a witness to what went on.

JOCASTA
A servant, the only one of the party
to escape.

OEDIPUS
He's still in service with you here?

JOCASTA
No. He brought us the news, but seeing you
in charge and grieving for Laius as he was,
he asked to be moved – grabbed me by the wrist,
and begged to be sent away: he was all
for the quiet life, somewhere out of town
would suit him best, he said. So I found him
a job as a shepherd. He was a good man.
It seemed the least kindness I could do him.

OEDIPUS
But you know where he is? If I wanted
to meet him, he could be brought here straight off?

JOCASTA
Yes, easily, but for what purpose?

OEDIPUS
I'm afraid to say more. I need to see him first.

JOCASTA
We'll send for him. But surely as your wife
I'm entitled to know what's troubling you.

OEDIPUS
You are, and I'll tell you. Who else would I tell?
I'm so far down the road to doom, I've nothing to lose.
My father was called Polybus, my mother
Merope. They lived well, I had a good childhood,
we were looked up to by everyone in town,
but then one day something very odd happened,
a little thing now I look back but at the time
I attached huge importance to it.
It was at a fancy dinner, a banquet.
One of the guests shouted from his cups
that I was not my father's son. Me, a bastard!
In a crack I lost it and went for him –
it needed twenty men to hold me back.
He's drunk, they said, ignore him, let it go.
But next day I had it out with my parents,
to make sure there was nothing behind his insult.
They were upset, naturally. Indignant too.
People like them aren't used to unpleasantness.
I felt guilty for having made them suffer
and relieved at the depth of their outrage.
And yet I couldn't put it behind me.
Rumours about my parentage spread like gorsefire.
The thought ate away at me more and more.
So without a word to my parents,
I set off one day at cock-light to the oracle,
where Apollo, worse luck, was happy to grant me
a private audience. Though he'd not confirm
what I'd come to ask, he'd other things as bad
to tell me – that I was doomed to sleep with
my mother and give her several children,
and before all this to murder my father.
Impossible, I said. Inevitable, he said.
He'd wager me all the happiness on earth.
  When I heard this, on the cold stone, I knew
I could never go back home. I took to the road,
sleeping rough, not caring where I ended up,
so long as I avoided my parents
and kept the gods from winning their bet.
One day on my wanderings I happened on the spot
where you say Laius met his death. A beck

running by, a drystone wall, a hawthorn tree
shaved slantwise by the wind: there I am,
sun beaming down, scrats of cloud in the sky,
minding my own, pondering which road to take,
when along comes a coach party – a driver,
two men on horseback, a messenger boy
running ahead, and a man inside the carriage,
just as you said. There's plenty room to pass,
but the driver and the bigwig inside
scream at me to clear out the bloody way.
If only they'd ask nicely I'd not mind,
but when the driver tries to force me off the road
I see red and fetch him one full in the face.
and then the old fellow inside the carriage
leans out and raddles me with a spiked club
or something, and keeps thumping me over the head
till I lose patience and learn him a lesson,
my blows are flisky little tigs, that's all,
but before I know it he's reeling under 'em,
he's rolling through the door of the carriage,
he's laid out on his back eyeing the heavens
and the body I'm battering is a corpse.
And then the others come at me, his servants,
wave on wave, every last mother's son of them
after my blood, and I've no choice, I let fly,
it's their lives or mine, next thing there's only me
left standing – the upshot is, they're all dead too.
  You see what that means: if the man in the carriage
was Laius, then Tiresias is right –
I am the source of this town's infection
and stand condemned to exile by my own law.
What a future I face – barred from every house,
despised, neglected, harried, spat at,
and all this because of orders I gave myself.
I am the man who laid a curse on his own life.
These hands you're holding killed your husband;
his blood stains the sheets where we lie together.
  Aren't the gods who chose that for me cruel?
What other word would fit? To set me up
to murder a man by accident,
and all just to prove who's boss and win a bet.
But I'll frustrate the bastards from collecting
their winnings. If need be, I'll go into the wilderness
again. Never never must I let them
best me and hit the jackpot of my shame.

CHORUS

There's no denying your story's ominous.
But until the witness confirms what he saw
you shouldn't start jumping to conclusions.

OEDIPUS

Yes, there's that shepherd. I've still one small thread
of hope.

JOCASTA

What's it you want of him, exactly?

OEDIPUS

If his story tallies with yours, I'm in the clear.

JOCASTA

I don't understand.

OEDIPUS

You said Laius was killed
by muggers – plural. If he confirms that,
then the killer can't have been me, can it?
A lone traveller is different from a gang.

JOCASTA

That's definitely how his story went.
Everyone heard him tell it, not just me.
He can't start chopping and changing it now.
He might tinker with the odd little detail,
but he'll not fulfil the prophecy *I* dread –
that Laius would be killed by a child of mine.
I've already told you how my poor son died
while still a baby. You're worrying needlessly.
There are ways of getting round the gods.
As to prophets, they've no more vision than a bat.

OEDIPUS

I'm with you there. I must see that shepherd, though.

JOCASTA

Trust me, I'll fix it. Come on, let's go.

exit OEDIPUS and JOCASTA

CHORUS

Let me be decent and honest
and stay within the law
and never have the nerve

to cheek the gods.
Just because we can't see them
don't mean they're not in charge.
Only a dulbert
would doubt or defy them.

It's arrogance creates a tyrant –
unchecked, a man will think
too much of himself
and go clambering sky-high cliffs
till he loses his footing
and the gods send him
hurtling to his death.
Aspiration's well and good.
Competition made this town
of ours what it is.
But arrogance we can do without.

Once a man takes a fancy to himself,
and puffs up like a thrush-chick,
and struts and preens
as though he owned the place,
not caring for justice,
scorning what others think
and thumbing his nose at the gods,
then he's headed for a pratfall
and deserves
every disaster he gets.

What kind of message would it be
if tyrants got away with tyranny?
We'd not bother to worship;
we'd never trust the gods again.

It's happening already.
Folk have begun to despair –
when's Zeus going to act?
why hasn't his promise been kept?
Laius was told on good account
that certain events
would come to pass.
Now no one believes they will.

The oracle won't keep its word.
The prophecies haven't come true.
The gods are on their way out.
Religion's disappearing from view.

enter JOCASTA

JOCASTA
I thought it wise to pay a little visit
to this altar – that's why I'm dressed up as I am.
If it weren't for Oedipus, I wouldn't bother
but he's worked himself into a lather
and needs all the help from me he can get –
can't sleep, won't eat, starts up at the slightest footfall,
and instead of being guided by experience
believes what the first man tells him, till the next man
tells him something else. I've tried to reason with him
but he won't listen. Perhaps you'll have more luck,
Apollo. I beg you to help us out.
We're a flock on the tops in a snow-storm
led by a shepherd who's gone howling mad.
You up there, I'm on my knees to you, look,
listen to me praying and guide us home!

enter a MESSENGER

MESSENGER
Can you show me to the house where Oedipus lives
or direct me to the man himself?

CHORUS
Look no further. This is his house. We know he's in.
The woman there's his wife and mother to his kids.

MESSENGER
Greetings – I can see Oedipus chose well.

JOCASTA
That's kind, stranger. But tell me what's brought you.

MESSENGER
I've a message to get to your husband.

JOCASTA
What message? Who sent you?

MESSENGER
I've come about Polybus.
It's good news, in the main, I think he'll be pleased –
though there's also a little bad news mixed in.

JOCASTA
I'm intrigued. What kind of news is both good and bad?

MESSENGER
The people back home want Oedipus
as their leader – so the word was when I left.

JOCASTA
But surely Polybus is their leader?

MESSENGER
He is. Or rather was, god rest his soul.

JOCASTA
What are you trying to say? That Polybus is dead?

MESSENGER
I'm not *trying* to say it, I am saying it.
Peacefully, in his sleep, a few days since.

JOCASTA
[exultant] There's another prophecy in the gutter:
how these soothsayers stay in business defeats me.
All these years Oedipus has been running
from his father, for fear of murdering him,
and now he's dead from natural causes –
and his son nowhere near when he breathed his last.

enter OEDIPUS

OEDIPUS
Why all the noise? What do you want, Jocasta?

JOCASTA
Listen to what this man has to tell you,
then ask yourself if you still believe in prophets.

OEDIPUS
I've never seen him before. What's he want?

JOCASTA
He's come a long way. He's brought a message
for you. Your father, Polybus, is dead.

OEDIPUS
What?
If it's true, let him say it in his own words.

MESSENGER
There is no other way to say it.
Your wife's right, I'm afraid – Polybus is dead.

OEDIPUS
How did he die? Nothing sinister, was it?

MESSENGER
You know how it is when folks are getting on.
There they are, health and sickness in the balance,
then a feather floats down and tips the scales.

OEDIPUS
Nothing out of the ordinary, then?
A common illness ...

MESSENGER
... aye, a common illness,
which because he was tottery finished him off.

OEDIPUS
[exultant] Aiiiieeeee! You're right, Jocasta, we've been kneeling
at the wrong altar. So much for prophecies,
so much for the little bird that said I'd kill him.
Half my life I've fretted when and where I'd do it,
and there he is, at rest under the earth,
and here am I, who never did him harm,
aside from upset him by leaving home
because of the oracle. Me murder my old man?
Death just crept up on him like a fog at night.
His corpse is milk-white, not even a scratch,
and the only sheets wrapped round him are those
on which a useless prophecy was written –
he took it with him, now it can never come true.

JOCASTA
Didn't I tell you all this ages since?

OEDIPUS
You did, but my fears tombed me in darkness.

JOCASTA
Now you can step out in the sunlight
and leave your fears behind.

OEDIPUS
Maybe – there's still the dread
of ending up in my mother's bed.

JOCASTA
Why should you dread it now? You brood too much,
my love. Life's a bran-tub – there's no knowing

what you'll pull out of it. It's all pot luck:
so take what you're given and live as best you can.
As to the thing you fear, forget it.
Most men have slept with their mothers in dreams,
it's a harmless fantasy. The best way's
to carry on as though it meant nothing.

OEDIPUS
I'd be happy to, if my mother were dust.
But since she's alive I can't relax, I must
stay on my guard.

JOCASTA
But all that's changed now.
Don't you feel better, knowing your father's dead?

OEDIPUS
Of course – but I'm still afraid of her bed.

MESSENGER
Who's this woman you're so worried about?

OEDIPUS
Merope – my mother – Polybus' widow.

MESSENGER
Why should a little old lady make you fearful?

OEDIPUS
Because of something the gods once told me.

MESSENGER
Is it a secret, or can anyone know?

OEDIPUS
I don't mind telling you. It was prophesied
I'd bed my mother, having first killed my father.
That's why all these years I've been avoiding them.
How else was I to get round the gods?
I don't complain; I've made a good life here.
But never to see your own parents is hard.

MESSENGER
Is that the only reason you've stayed away?
Because of your mother?

OEDIPUS
My father too.

MESSENGER
I should be kicking myself, then. I came here
to do you a good turn; if only I'd known,
I could have done you a second good turn
and put your mind at rest.

OEDIPUS

At rest? Do that
and I'll pay you whatever you ask.

MESSENGER
Well, I didn't trudge all this way from charity.
I hoped, if you came back with me, to be rewarded.

OEDIPUS
But I can't return with my mother alive ...

MESSENGER
That's my point, you're under a delusion.

OEDIPUS
I don't understand. You mean she's dead too?

MESSENGER
No, but if she's the reason you won't come back ...

OEDIPUS
The prophecy ... How many times must I spell it out?

MESSENGER
But the point is you've nothing to fear from her.

OEDIPUS
As long as I'm her son, I'll go on worrying.

MESSENGER
But that's what I'm telling you – you're *not* her son.

OEDIPUS
Merope's not my mother? What about Polybus, then?

MESSENGER
He's less claim to be your dad than I have.

OEDIPUS
You! But I've not even met you till today.

MESSENGER
You're getting in a muddle. I'm not your dad.

But the nub is: nor's Polybus, neither.

OEDIPUS
So why did he tell everyone I was his son?

MESSENGER
I gave you to him when you were a baby,
with my own hands.

OEDIPUS
You handed me over?
And yet they loved me like their own son.

MESSENGER
They'd tried to have children but they couldn't:
with no brood of their own, of course they loved you.

OEDIPUS
So what were you doing with me in the first place?
Was I sold off like a lump of meat?
Did you pick me up from a market-stall?

MESSENGER
I was up on the tops, close to a wood,
and there you were, I stumbled on you.

OEDIPUS
A strange spot to be in – were you passing through?

MESSENGER
I had a summer job looking after sheep.

OEDIPUS
You trekked about and took what work came along?

MESSENGER
Finding you was the best day's work I ever did.

OEDIPUS
What state was I in? poorly? injured?

MESSENGER
Those feet of yours have the answer to that.

OEDIPUS
Why drag them into it?

MESSENGER
They still bear the scars,

that's why. They'd been pierced with rusty nails
then bound together with a rope – I had to cut you free.

OEDIPUS
My badge of shame.

MESSENGER
Aye, the kids used to tease you.
"Oedipus, Legs full of pus, Can't-Run-With-Us":
it's there in your name and your nicknames.

OEDIPUS
Instead of presents, my parents gave me wounds.
Instead of lopping my foreskin, they bored holes
into my ankles. What kind of people were they?

MESSENGER
I don't know. You'd have to ask the man
who brought you to me.

OEDIPUS
But I thought you found me.
I thought you said you handed me over.

MESSENGER
I did find you – in his arms. And I did
hand you over – after he handed you to me.

OEDIPUS
Who was he? What's his name? Do you know him?

MESSENGER
From what I could make out, he worked for Laius.

OEDIPUS
You mean the same Laius who was leader here?

MESSENGER
That's right – this feller was one of his herdsmen.

OEDIPUS
If he's alive, I want to meet him. Where is he?

MESSENGER
I don't know, I'm not from round here. Ask these people.

OEDIPUS
Do you know the man he means? Is he about
anywhere? Come on, let's be hearing from you.

CHORUS
It's the same man you were asking to see,
the shepherd who's already been sent for.
But you'd best ask Jocasta – she knows more.

OEDIPUS
Do you? Is the man this man's talking about
the man we've sent for?

JOCASTA
This man, that man,
the other man – God knows which man he means.
Pay him no attention: he'll get you nowhere.

OEDIPUS
But these are pictures in my life story,
they're evidence, they're clues to the mystery.

JOCASTA
Some mysteries are best left unsolved.
The fuss people make about finding themselves –
who we are's what we make of our lives
not who our parents are. If you've any sense,
you'll not pursue this – I've suffered enough.

OEDIPUS
Why should you suffer? *Your* ancestry's secure.
The lines on *your* brow run back centuries.
If it turns out my mother and her mother
were slaves, that I'm a slum-kid three times over,
it won't be any skin off *your* nose,
it won't make the blood in *your* veins any less blue.

JOCASTA
I beg you, Oedipus, leave it at that.

OEDIPUS
I'll only leave it when I've untied the knot.

JOCASTA
What about our knot? You'll destroy us.
When I say stop, it's for the best, believe me.

OEDIPUS
I'm sick of being told what's best for me.
Let me be the judge of that.

JOCASTA
You're a poor judge, then:

if you do find out who you are, you'll regret it.

OEDIPUS
I'm a free man. I'll do what I like.
Where's that shepherd? Fetch him here at once,
and let my wife stew in her noble juice.

JOCASTA
You miserable fool. I'd have preferred
a kinder epitaph, but that's my last word.

exit JOCASTA

CHORUS
What's wrong with her? She's building up a dam
of silence for herself, when behind it
there's a river of pain.

OEDIPUS
Well, let it flood out,
if it has to. And if there's so much pus breaks loose
I'm swept away in its torrent, so be it,
I've still a right to find out who I am.
A woman of her class might be ashamed
on my behalf if it turns out I'm low-born,
but I consider myself to be lucky.
I was born into a family called Chance –
there's my father, he's one Chance, and my mother,
she's another, and all my brother Chances,
and my sisters, and my cousins as well,
and whether their house is humble or grand
doesn't matter, I need to track it down –
it's the only place I'll ever call home.
Yes, I'm happy to take what Chances come along.
I am the man I am, and no altering it,
so I might as well discover all I can.

CHORUS
Your ours, Oedipus,
you're the man.
We'll soon find out
which neck of the woods
you come from,
but no matter what place,
no matter which parents,
they're all from God's own country
so let's sing and dance

and claim you as ours.

Who was your mother,
Oedipus, and who your dad?
which long-legged doe was it
mated with which goatish lad?
there's a stud called Pan
many a lass has spread her thighs for –
was it him, or was it Hermes,
king of the snickets?
Or Dionysus maybe,
luring some nymph
up on the fells with him
and laying her down
in his fern and heather bed?

Were you the outcome
of a lifelong passion
or a one-night stand?
was your mother
a randy daughter of Loxias?
a poor whore working an alley?
a straying wife put in the club
by cocky Apollo?
or a virgin learning the ropes
under the gaze
of a chalk-white moon?

It's a mystery.
But not a tragedy.
Whatever the answer,
the birth was human,
the labour-pains mortal,
the child squishy and raw.
You're our man, Oedipus.
Whoever your parents,
we'll sing and dance
and claim you as ours.

enter a SHEPHERD, formerly the servant of Laius

OEDIPUS
Now then – I'll wager my life that's the shepherd
we've been looking for.
[to one of CHORUS] Tell me, aren't I right?

CHORUS
Aye, that's him. He was working for Laius

in those days – a simple soul, happier with sheep
than with people, but a man you can trust.

OEDIPUS
[to MESSENGER] Is this the man *you* meant, too?

MESSENGER

It is, no question,
you're looking at him.

OEDIPUS

Tell me, my friend,
were you once a worker for Laius?

SHEPHERD
I was. Not the fly-by or seasonal kind,
neither – I practically grew up in his house.

OEDIPUS
What kind of work did you do for him?

SHEPHERD
Most of the time I were looking after sheep.

OEDIPUS
Where was this?

SHEPHERD

Not too far off, up on the tops.

OEDIPUS
And this man here – do you remember him?

SHEPHERD
What's he got to do with it?

OEDIPUS

Did you never
come across him?

SHEPHERD

Not so it's stuck in my mind.

MESSENGER
No wonder, he wouldn't want it to stick.
But maybe I can freshen his memory.
For three summers – that's each May to each backend –
we worked on next-door farms; he had two flocks

cropping at the tussocks, and I had one.
Many's the sun-up we'd have a natter.
Many's the clipping time we sharpened shears together.
He used to wear a brown shirt and trousers,
the same shade as doddings on the rumps of sheep.
Now I defy him to have forgotten all that.

SHEPHERD
It rings a bell, aye, but only faintly.

MESSENGER
Well, you'll not forget a certain present
you once gave me – a child to bring up as my own.

SHEPHERD
What if I did?

MESSENGER
That child's this man in front of you.

SHEPHERD
Shut your trap. I don't want to know about it.
Another word from you and I'll ...

OEDIPUS
Don't blame *him*.
If anyone's at fault here, it's you.

SHEPHERD
Me? What have I done?

OEDIPUS
The minute he mentions
a child, you lose your temper with him.

SHEPHERD
He's talking tripe, that's why. He's out of his depth.

OEDIPUS
It's me he's answering to; I'm in charge here.
You were asked nicely. But we've other ways ...

SHEPHERD
I'm an old man with a dicky heart – don't threaten me
or you'll have a corpse on your hands.

OEDIPUS
We'll risk it.

SHEPHERD
I can feel my ticker going – what's it you want?

OEDIPUS
Did you or didn't you hand him a baby?

SHEPHERD
I did – though I'd rather've been pecked to death
by ravens.

OEDIPUS
There's still time to arrange that,
if you don't tell us the truth.

SHEPHERD
It'll be death
for me any road. I've had an hunch lately
I'm not long for this world.

MESSENGER
Hark at him tantling on.
He's not wraithly, he's just playing for time.

SHEPHERD
I said I gave him the kid – what more do you want?

OEDIPUS
Where did the baby come from? Was it yours?

SHEPHERD
It was given me. ...

OEDIPUS
Given you? *Who* gave it you?

SHEPHERD
The loudest voices at a fair are hawkers
with nowt on their stalls. I'm stopping shut.

OEDIPUS
I won't ask you again. Spit it out now
or I'll stop you shut for good.

SHEPHERD
The kid came
from Laius' house.

OEDIPUS
Was it a chance-bairn?

Was its mother one of the maids?

SHEPHERD

I want to speak,
but I'm staring down into a huge black quarry
and I can't bring myself to leap off.

OEDIPUS
I'm there beside you, I can see the blackness
looming up at me. But I must hear you say it.

SHEPHERD
The child was Laius', so I were told.
But your wife could give you a fuller picture.

OEDIPUS
So it was my wife who gave you the child?

SHEPHERD
Aye.

OEDIPUS
Telling you what?

SHEPHERD
That I was to kill it.

OEDIPUS
She was its mother, yet she had the heart ...

SHEPHERD
She was afraid of the prophecy, that's why.

OEDIPUS
The prophecy ...

SHEPHERD
They reckoned once the child
grew up it were due to kill its father.

OEDIPUS
So you were meant to get rid of it
but instead you gave it to this man here. Why?

SHEPHERD
This heart of mine were weak even back then.
I knew he hailed from the back of beyond
and I thought he'd take it home with him,
so we'd not see hide nor hair of it again.

Only he found it a good home and helped it come back
to haunt us. To chop it up would have been kinder,
for if you're the man he says you are, you're nowt,
or worse than – you were born to fry in hell.

OEDIPUS

All true. Every worst dread, every last detail,
dragged out of the darkness and exposed.
Let me stand here in the sunlight one last time,
shown up for what I am – bad seed, birth defect,
murderer, marriage-breaker, widow-maker,
in-breeder, plague germ, agent of genocide.
You're right: I'm not nowt, me, I'm worse than nowt –
I was cursed, I didn't stand a chance,
they pinned me like a rat under a pitchfork.
But that's how I'll go down in history: Oedipus,
the man who killed his father and fucked his mum.

exit OEDIPUS

CHORUS

Generation on generation
living only to die,
men and women
thrown like dice
into the wheel of fortune,
dancing and skipping
as if they could forever
ride their luck,
then losing their speed
and clattering to a halt.

This game they call life –
is it worth the toss?
I've done the sums
and I don't think so.
You think you're winning,
but it's an illusion.
There's only one number
with your name on it,
with everyone's name,
and that's death.

Take Oedipus.
If ever a man seemed
to have luck on his side
it was him. The gods smiled,

they dealt him the best cards,
there was nothing he lacked.
So if even Oedipus
can end up unhappy,
where does that leave us?
His fate must also be ours.

Fame, riches,
a good marriage.
He beat the Sphinx.
He saved our skins.
He banished death.
Hero, healer,
father, leader,
no one was held
in more esteem.

Look at him now,
his world turned upside down.
Is there a sadder story?
In ignorance razing
his father's wheat and
ploughing his mother's furrow
– how could the gods
laike with him so long
and not weep to see
his suffering?

Poor Oedipus. Time,
which knows everything,
has caught you unawares.
The silly murder,
the sham marriage,
the misbegotten kids –
you hadn't a clue,
you were innocent
yet guilty as hell.
A charmed life,
but now the charm's worn off
and the gods
have got their way.

If only, Oedipus –
that's your lament.
Mine too: if only
I'd never set eyes on you.

Once I wrote eulogies
for you; this is an elegy.
Life and hope
were the tunes
I used to sing;
now it's death and despair
you bring.

If only we could stay
immaculate and unborn.
The next best bet's
an early burial
and eternal rest.
Poor Oedipus:
I'm singing a dirge
over your open coffin.
I lay my fingers
on your eyes,
on my own eyes too,
and close the lids.

enter a SERVANT

SERVANT
My friends, you don't know what you're in for –
there are things to tell you, and sights I've seen,
which will crush you like boots treading on daisies.
If all the rivers in the world joined up,
they'd still not wash the blood clean from the accident.
I say accident – but what kills me is that
it were done on purpose.

CHORUS
We thought we'd drained
our cup of misery – don't say there's more.

SERVANT
There is – but since you're mired in horrors
I'll not drag it out. Jocasta is dead.

CHORUS
Jocasta? Why her? How can that be?

SERVANT
Think yourself lucky you weren't there to see it, like me.
I'll tell you what went on as best I can.
First she rushes from here, we all know that.

And once across the threshhold, and through the hall,
she flies straight to the bedroom, tearing her hair out
as she goes. She slams the door behind her,
so we can't see, but we know she's on her knees
and we can hear her crying out for Laius,
maybe hoping to summon his ghost,
and reminiscing about their only child,
who murdered him and left her a widow
and then slid into her bed and planted his seed
so that a crop of skanky blooms sprang up –
and all the while she's hammering her fists
against her marriage-bed, berating it
for playing host to monstrous lusts and labours,
and for allowing her to conceive
a husband by her husband, children by her child.
  How she made her last arrangements I'm not sure,
because next thing Oedipus bursts in,
distracting us from her sorrows with his own –
he's like a wild man, rampaging about the house,
ordering us to tell him where his wife is,
though she's no more his wife than his mother.
And as he stands there, suddenly it hits him –
it's none of us who lets on, it must be a god
telling him, because a scream rises from him
like a curlew drawing power down from the heavens,
and with a strength way beyond his own
he hurls himself at her bedroom's double doors,
bends the metal bolts with his bare hands,
forces the door from its hinges and flings it open:
which is when we see her hanging there, like a crow
or vixen some farmer had snared and strung up – bare throat,
rope coiled round her neck, body gently twisting
in the breeze from her bedroom window. Jocasta!
A bitter sob tears Oedipus' mouth open
as he seizes her body, cuts it down
and lays her gently on the floor in front of him,
as though to hug and kiss her back to life
or worship the white body that bore him.
Then suddenly – to me this is the worst part –
he rips the golden brooch from the neck of her dress
and lovingly fondles the pin that held it there,
then turns the pin towards his face, crying out
against his eyes for all the suffering they've caused.
"What help have you been to me?" he shouts.
"You've led me to people I shouldn't have loved,
and taken me from those I did. Never again.

It's time to dwell forever in the dark."
Then he lifts his hand, tips his head back
and stabs himself in the eyes again and again.
With each new lunge another stream of blood
rolls down till his face is a beck in spate
and his cheeks are a rockspout gushing red.
So there we have them, joined together
to the last, one living, the other dead,
one laid out like a slab of white marble,
the other a waterfall of foaming red.
They were happy once, and called themselves man and wife.
What names now fit them best – doomed, disgraced,
wedded to catastrophe? Any will do.
They hit the jackpot – all the griefs are theirs.

CHORUS

Where's Oedipus now? What's he doing?

SERVANT

He's told his servants to throw the doors open
so all the town can queue up and meet the monster –
the man who killed his dad and who ... well, I'll not
use his word for what he did to his mam.
He says it's people's last chance to see him
because he's flitting the minute he can –
so the curse will lift and the plague go with him.
But I can't imagine how he'll get round
without a guide, and the pain must be terrible.
See for yourself – if you don't soften
your hearts are more granite than mine.

enter OEDIPUS, blinded

OEDIPUS

You savage gods up there, where are you
leading me this time? I know I'm not dead yet,
or my voice wouldn't be bouncing off the walls.

CHORUS

God, he's a mess.
I've seen some sights
in my time
but none like this.

OEDIPUS

I'm wrapped in a cloud, I'm under the waves.
If I keep walking I might get lucky

and fall through the trapdoor to oblivion.

CHORUS
What was he thinking of?
He must have been
off his head.
I can't stand to look.

OEDIPUS
My eyes are like meat-knives stabbing at my skull,
but the memories locked inside them are worse –
all the sights cupped in my empty sockets.

CHORUS
There are questions
I'd like to ask him
but if that means
staring him in the face –
no, I can't do it.

OEDIPUS
Is that you? Yes, it is, I know it is:
if I had eyes I'd weep in gratitude
that you're here beside me, despite everything.

CHORUS
How could you do it?
Where did you find the guts?
Was it inside you,
or did it come from somewhere else?

OEDIPUS
All that's happened was decided by the gods.
Except the last bit: that was my own idea.
Why bother hanging on to my eyes,
when all I'll ever see is misery?

CHORUS
It's a good question.

OEDIPUS
What's left for me?
what sight or sound can cheer, what hand warm mine,
what greeting touch my heart? Take me away
from my friends, friends – I'm not fit company for you.
Even the gods hate me, now they've finished
playing tomcat and left me like a dormouse
in the dust.

CHORUS

It's a double load – the pain
in your body, the agonies in your head.

OEDIPUS

I blame the man who untied my ankles.
Oh, he reckoned he was doing me a favour.
But think of the griefs he could have spared others
if he'd not spared me. He ought to die for that.

CHORUS

You're right – if only he'd left you there.

OEDIPUS

Then I'd not have come here with my father's blood
still leaking from my hands, nor have tied the knot
with the woman I was roped to in the womb.
Now the gods up in their loft are counting
their winnings, and laugh down at me in contempt
– father-killer, mother-fucker, dupe.

CHORUS

I'd be lying if I said you did right
to yank out your eyes; you'd be better off dead
than living your days through in a black pit.

OEDIPUS

I'm sick of being told what's right and wrong.
This blindness won't only get me through life,
it'll be a comfort when I'm dead;
because how can I look my parents
in the eyes when I meet them on the far side?
or bear the sight of my children, in this life?
And this town that's been my home for years,
with its towers and alleys and altars,
what do you think it means to me now? Only this –
that I must abide by my own law and leave,
since I'm guilty of infecting it with the plague.
  Wrong to blind myself? If I knew a method
to make myself deaf, I'd use that too,
and shut my senses down one by one
till eyes, ears, nose and tongue were blocked off
and all touch gone in my flesh and fingers.
  Why was the night so mild when I was left?
I was a weak, mewling bundle – a wolf,
even a fox or crow, could have had me
for breakfast. When the midwives and neighbours

cooed over me in my cradle back home,
why didn't they see the filth under the blanket?
Oh, and that place where the three roads meet,
with the beck running by, and the drystone wall,
and the hawthorn tree shaved slantwise by the wind,
does it remember me and the blood I sprayed
across the grass, does it still look the same
or has it been altered by what I did there?
How wide has the stain of guilt spread, how deep
has it soaked in? Will anyone believe in
marriage now? I was conceived in marriage,
I seemed pure, but my seed was a bad seed,
I went swimming back up the birth canal,
I knocked at the same door I'd entered by,
I docked at the same harbour I set out from,
I re-opened the old wound that bled me,
I sowed myself again and again,
I made fathers, brothers, sons, daughters, sisters
and mothers in my image, a whole family
locked in on itself, slopping at its own banks,
a blocked drain, a wishing well gone putrid,
a standing rockpool of eels and crabs.
All that ugliness stemmed from my spunk.
So come on, grab hold and get me out of here.
Don't worry, I won't be heavy to carry:
I'm the lighter by two eyeballs, and though
my evil's massive it doesn't weigh an ounce.

enter CREON

CHORUS
Here's Creon, let him decide what to do.
He'll know – he's the gaffer now.

OEDIPUS
Creon!
Why should he listen, after how I treated him?

CREON
[to OEDIPUS] I've not come to crow or dwell on the past.
[to the CHORUS] But if any of you here have lost faith
in your fellow men, let me remind you
the gods are still there and deserve our respect.
Which is why you must get him inside at once
and not shame the earth we stand on or the sun
that lights us or the rain that washes our skin.
No messing, take him in, it's private business now

which only family should be present for.

OEDIPUS
Don't take me in, Creon. Send me somewhere
I'll not meet a soul from one year to the next.

CREON
Believe me, I'd have done it already
if it were in my keeping. But there's a god
to consult – I need to know what he says.

OEDIPUS
You do know! He laid it all out to you.
Whoever killed Laius should be killed or exiled.

CREON
That was it, roughly, but we have to check,
we must follow the gods to the letter.
I know even you believe in the gods.

OEDIPUS
Of course: after all they've put me through,
I couldn't not. But I've something else
to ask, too – that you'll do right by the woman
lying dead in there, who's your sister after all
and deserves a proper burial.
And then my children – that's another question.
I don't mean my sons, Creon, no need to fret
about them, they'll find the means to make a life.
But my poor daughters, who know no other father,
who I've watched over since they were born,
who eat with me each day – promise you'll look after them.
And will you bring them now, so I can hold them?
Take pity, Creon – if I can touch them again
it'll be as though these fingers were my eyes.

enter ANTIGONE and ISMENE

They're here already, aren't they? I can hear them
crying, my two sweet daughters, thank you Creon,
you've brought them to see me, aren't I right?

CREON
I know what they've always meant to you.

OEDIPUS
Come here, my little ones, don't be frightened,
let your father touch you, your brother too,
who lost his eyes from having loved too much.

Yes, I'm blind. How else could I have spawned you
in the self-same waters that spawned me?
The channel I splashed through as a baby
I returned to as a man, riding the tide,
and you rose like lovely dolphins in my wake.
  These sockets are empty, but when I think
how you'll be punished because of me,
I can feel my eyes water and weep.
All the gatherings you'll rush home early from,
the fetes, banquets, wedding parties and dances
where you'll be taunted for who and what you are.
And when you reach the age for getting wed,
what man will have the guts to be your husband?
Because let's not pretend it doesn't stink.
Your father with these hands killed his father.
Your father with these hands seduced his mother
and sowed his seed in the soil where he was sown
and from that seed grew the blossoms that are you –
beautiful flowers, but who'll want to pick you?
You'll be thrown in a ditch and left to rot.
  Listen, Creon, their parents are finished,
it's up to you to be their father now:
take good care, keep them from poverty
and prostitution, don't let them sink like me.

CREON
Come on. Enough. Inside.

OEDIPUS
                                        No. There's a place
on the tops where my parents meant me to die
– send me there and let me haunt my own grave.

CREON
I've told you – it's for the gods to decide.

OEDIPUS
Why should they bother to help? They hate me.

CREON
All right, have it your way, I give my consent.
Let go of your children and we'll be off.

OEDIPUS
No, don't take them from me, no, no, no, no.

CREON
Let go. You're not in charge any more – I am.

Accept it, brother, your days of power are gone.

exit OEDIPUS, CREON, children and attendants

CHORUS
Citizens, good people, think on Oedipus.
He it was who solved the Sphinx's riddle,
ruled this town for many years, and was revered
and envied by all. Now look at him, struck down
and doomed to wander on some far black hill
till death puts him out his misery.
As we sit waiting for our own good night,
remember it's only then we'll be all right.
The gods are cruel but the gods are just –
no man can be reckoned happy till he's dust.

ANTIGONE

by Sophocles
a version by Blake Morrison, 2003

CHARACTERS

ANTIGONE, daughter of Oedipus and Jocasta

ISMENE, her sister

CREON, newly appointed leader, brother of Jocasta

HAEMON, his son

EURYDICE, his wife

TIRESIAS, a prophet

A GUARD

A MESSENGER

CHORUS of men

Antigone was first performed at Salts Mill, Saltaire, Bradford on 7th October 2003 with the following Northern Broadsides cast:

Chorus/Guard/Messenger	Conrad Nelson
Chorus/Tiresias	Andrew Vincent
Chorus/Haemon	Jonathan Le Billon
Chorus	Andrew Whitehead
Chorus	Dennis Conlon
Chorus	David Bowen
Chorus	Jason Furnival
Antigone	Sally Carman
Ismene	Sara Poyzer
Creon	Barrie Rutter
Eurydice	Jacqueline Redgewell
Director	Barrie Rutter
Designers	Giuseppe Belli and Emma Barrington-Binns
Composer	Conrad Nelson

By the town wall. Dawn. A CHORUS of townsfolk (male) are celebrating victory.

CHORUS

The sun, the sun!
Here comes the biggest sun
that ever dawned,
striding red-faced over the hills,
burning off night's stubble,
shining for us like yesterday
when it picked out the enemy
at our gates,
our seven gates,
and fired us up
to clatter and skelp them,
till they turned and ran
like a river under a bridge,
the sun, the sun,
our secret weapon,
our seven-day wonder,
seven days a week!

Seven!
Seven sentries in seven turrets.
Seven blasts from seven trumpets.
Seven battles at seven gates.

They sneaked up at first light,
like a kestrel
hanging on the hill,
poised to plunge
and make a kill,

hungry as a bloodhound
that's not been fed in weeks,
foaming at the mouth
and slavering to sink
their teeth in our necks,

an enemy black with evil
but carrying white shields,
waiting to stain
their lime-fresh battledress
with our blood.

But we were ready for them.

We snuffed the flames
when they torched our towers,
we drove them back
when their swords flashed,
we sent them packing
from all seven gates.

Seven!

It's Zeus we have to thank,
Zeus!
When Zeus hears a man brag
he comes down on him
like a rockfall in a quarry.
And when he saw
that showoff army
swanning down the valley
he kicked up a storm,
sending hail to sting their eyes,
and wind to shred their banners,
and the best he saved for last,
letting a soldier of theirs
scale our walls to the top
then hurling forked lightning
as he swanked in triumph,
so his ladder was yanked away
and his foot slipped
and he toppled from the tower
and fell like a firework
to fizzle out at the feet
of his friends –

friends whose ends
proved as bad or worse
when we poured from the gates
– our seven gates! –
to join the fight.
Every man of theirs
was hacked to bits –
two arms, two legs, one head,
one body, and one cock –

and then we learned
how little spunk they had.

1-2-3-4-5-6-7.

Seven fighters and seven cowards.
Seven hawks and seven chickens.
Seven bodies in seven bits.

It was us against them
and we thrashed them
seven-nil.

It was us against them,
except in one scrap
it was us against us.

Polyneices, the son of Oedipus:
there he was, one of ours,
fighting for them.

Eteocles took him on.
Someone had to.
Oedipus' other son.
Brother against brother.

A fight to death.
Unnatural.
It takes the gloss off.
It drops you flat.
Don't dwell on that.
Death's behind us now.
It's peace not war.
Let's drink to Dionysus.
We'll sup seven flagons
in his name.

Seven!
Seven generals on seven stallions.
Seven warriors with seven weapons.
Seven victories at seven gates.
Seven!

enter ANTIGONE and ISMENE

ANTIGONE
We're one, aren't we, you and me? We're sisters,
indivisible, flesh and blood.

ISMENE
Of course.

ANTIGONE
What a legacy: we've had the lot.
Ruin, misery, disaster, disgrace:
It's all our father left us in his will.
And now the war's over, have you heard?
Creon's new law. A law passed to shaft our family.
The whole town's on about it. Don't look so blank.

ISMENE
I'm not like you – I keep my head down.
Good news or bad: what's it matter either way?
We lost two brothers in one day – that's all I know.
Yeh, yeh, the enemy's been sent packing.
As if I care. No, I've heard nothing, me.

ANTIGONE
That's why I brought you here, alone,
to put our heads together. You need to know.

ISMENE
What is it?

ANTIGONE
Our two brothers, that's what.
One of them's to be buried with honours,
while the other's left to rot.

ISMENE
Eteocles ...

ANTIGONE
He's to get the full treatment.
He'll be laid under a slab as a war hero.

ISMENE
And Polyneices ...

ANTIGONE
No such eulogy for him.
He's to lie where he fell, on the hard grey earth.
And if rooks land to peck his eyes out,
and worms slide through his ears, and a passing fox
makes off with a kidney or slice of liver,
till all that's left is bare bones, so be it –
we can't bury him, that's Creon's new law.
And to show he means it, he's fixed a penalty –
disobey and we'll be stoned to death.
So now you know. Family pride's at stake.

This is one gob on our honour we'll not take.

ISMENE
But laws are laws. If those are Creon's orders,
what am I meant to do?

ANTIGONE
Share the load.
We'll do it together, as sisters.

ISMENE
Do what together?

ANTIGONE
Bury Polyneices.

ISMENE
When a law's been passed to prevent us?

ANTIGONE
He's our brother. We can't abandon him now.
Men are brutes, they can't be trusted
with bodies. We're women. We know what's right.

ISMENE
But that's madness. Creon's forbidden it.

ANTIGONE
It'd be madness to give in to him.
He's no right to destroy our family.

ISMENE
We'll destroy it, if we resist him.
Think of Oedipus, our father. You saw –
how he ended up hated and disgraced,
stabbing his eyes out rather than face his crimes,
doomed to wander on some far black hill
till death put him out of his misery.
And his wife, our mother, *his* mother,
knotting a rope round her throat to stop the grief.
And now our brothers, fighting till their blood ran out,
drained dry as two calves on a butcher's hook.
That leaves just us, last of the batch. If we break
Creon's law, the family will be finished.
Yes, we're women, but women aren't built
to do battle. Men's wills are like iron.
To live with them, women have to give,
like flower-stems bending in the wind.
That's why we should submit to Creon

even if his law is wrong. It's common sense,
it's survival – Polyneices would understand.
Do as we're told and we'll save our necks.

ANTIGONE

I won't waste my breath trying to persuade you.
Even if you said you'd changed your mind,
I'd not let you help me bury him now. No,
I'll do it on my own, and when they pound me
like raw meat, when they batter me with stones,
I'll feel no pain from the blows, only joy –
my body will be lying next to my brother's,
we'll snuggle together in his grave.
The living can look out for themselves,
it's the dead we should cling to and cherish,
since it's them we have to live with when we're gone
and that's longer than we'll ever spend here.
The laws of the gods are what we live by –
if we break them, we deserve to die.

ISMENE

I'd never dishonour the gods. But to wreak
havoc on Creon's law – I can't, I'm too weak.

ANTIGONE

You stay here like a good little girl then.
I'm off to bury our brother.

ISMENE

It's dangerous. I'm worried for you.

ANTIGONE

It's yourself you should be worrying for.

ISMENE

Tell no one. Then they'll not know it's you.
I promise to keep it a secret, too.

ANTIGONE

Keep it a secret? Tell everyone you meet!
Get out there and shout it in the street.

ISMENE

Why waste the effort? You're bound to fail.

ANTIGONE

I'm bound to fail if I don't try. You can't stop me.
No one can. They'll have to kill me first.

ISMENE
What does Polyneices care what happens
to his body, now he's dead? It's madness.

ANTIGONE
Shut your mouth, before I start to hate you –
before our poor brother starts to hate you, too.
You say I'm mad. But to betray those we love
and ought to honour – that isn't sanity.
Let them stone me if they want. I'd rather that
than eke out my days as a scuttling rat.

exit ANTIGONE

ISMENE
Go and do it, then. You're mad as the wind –
a danger to yourself, to others too.
But you're my sister, and I love you.

exit ISMENE

CHORUS
To those we love ... and those who love us ...
and those that love them that love those
that love them that love us
... to all seven of us!
Seven!

Seven wars and seven warriors.
Seven revels and seven revellers.
Seven victories at seven gates.

But only one Dionysus.
Dionysus!
It was Zeus who won the war for us
But Dionysus will win the peace.

Seven songs and seven singers.
Seven jigs and seven dancers.
Seven flagons and seven wines.

Dionysus!
We won the war by using all our muscles.
In peace we'll get our pleasures from just one.

Seven lads and seven lasses!
Seven beds and seven pillows!
Seven times a night!

Shush –
Creon's coming.
Creon!
He's the man.
Our Coalition leader.
Our peacekeeper.
Our heroes' hero.
Our new number one.
What's he want?

enter CREON

CREON
Friends, the world turned upside down for a day,
but victory's ours. There have been losses –
I've suffered them with you. Good men have died.
Precious sons have been sacrificed in the cause.
But let nothing spoil this moment of triumph.
We did the job. The terrorists are dead,
their cells wiped out, their weapons seized. We shocked them
with our courage. They ran from us in awe.
And in the seedtime of peace and prosperity
it's my duty, as leader, to address you.
  I know how loyal you've been to this town
through its long history. How well you served Laius,
till he was murdered; and stuck by Oedipus,
when he was in charge; and after he went
rallied round his sons. Now those sons have gone too,
both in one day, each taking out the other –
a terrible loss, unnatural, repellent,
leaving a hole at the top, which I,
as next of kin, have stepped in to fill.
  Friends, there's no saying how good a leader
will be till he's proved himself in the job.
But this much I do know: if he's too cowardly
to say what he believes, and fails to do
what's right for fear of making himself unpopular –
then he's useless. The interests of the state
always come first, ahead of friends and family.
If our security is under threat,
if foreigners are scuttling through our gates
and your lives are at risk, then I tell you –
you'd not thank me for keeping my trap shut.
Only when we're secure can we afford
to be open and trusting – that's my belief.
It's a wonderful town we live in

because stone walls and iron laws protect it.
But we must remain vigilant at all times.
That's why I've passed a new law, concerning
Oedipus' two sons. The first of them,
Eteocles, who laid down his life for us,
shall be buried with full military honours.
We'll have a cenotaph built, and a statue carved,
and you can line up to pay your respects –
lay flowers, burn candles or shout his name
to the gods, so he's never forgotten.
But as for the other, his so-called brother,
Polyneices, who was born here, buggered off,
married some foreign tart then came back
armed to the hilt as a mercenary,
who planned to kill his family and destroy our town,
whose dream was to make slaves of men like you
and might have done it but for your courage
at the seven gates –

CHORUS

Seven!

CREON

– as for our enemy,
he's to be left where he fell, unburied and unmourned,
his only visitors magpies and mongrels
on the lookout for scraps – let them stuff themselves
on his liver and guts, it's what he deserves.
Let no man ever say of me that I rate
a traitor above a patriot. It's men like you,
to whom this town means more than even your kin,
who'll be honoured in this world and the next.

CHORUS

If that's how you want it, to treat one brother one way
and the other another, we can't argue.
It's your right, as leader. You make the laws.
We only keep them.

CREON

I'm hoping for your help
not just in keeping this law but in enforcing it.

CHORUS

You'd be better off asking someone younger ...
These eyes of mine aren't as sharp as they were ...
We've enough on without burdens like that.

CREON
I'm not asking you to be watchmen.
I've already posted men to guard the corpse.

CHORUS
So what are you asking? What would our job be?

CREON
Not to shelter any law-breaker, that's all.

CHORUS
We're not daft. We know it's death for us if we do.

CREON
True enough. But once money's involved ...
You know how men's eyes light up at the thought.

enter GUARD

GUARD
I'd be lying if I said I'm out of breath
from legging it. It's not far, and all downhill,
and they told me to be quick, but I'd not break
into a run. Even walking, I kept stopping.
Several times I turned back. The path was smooth,
it was my head that kept jarring and twisting.
I had these two voices drilling into me.
"You daft sod," goes one, in my right ear,
"What's the hurry? Keep on walking like that
and you'll land up in your own grave."
"What you hanging about for?" goes the other,
in the left. "It's your job to tell Creon.
If you dawdle, and he hears the news
from someone else, he'll have you lashed to death."
I can't decide if I'm coming or going.
"Stop where you are", "Get a move on, sharpish",
"Take a break", "Sprint to the finishing line":
I like a spot of company on a trip,
but this is me banging on to myself,
and though I don't have many miles to come
all the dithering turns it into a marathon.
At last one voice gets the better of the ding-dong,
bullying me to come here and tell you.
And if I'm murdered for my pains, well stuff it:
the gods must have decreed my face don't fit.

CREON
What are you burbling about? Get to the point.

GUARD
First off, I'm worried I'll get in trouble.
I didn't do it, and didn't see who did,
so by rights I can't be blamed or punished.
All the same ...

CREON
                    I can't see where this is going.
You're throwing so many words at us all
they've collapsed and buried you, like a wall.

GUARD
Carrying bad news is like having the squitters –
you don't want people to know, you hold it in
as long as you can.

CREON
                    Enough! Just tell your story.

GUARD
The corpse. Somebody has buried the corpse.
Not a proper burial, six foot under –
just a skim of earth over the body
to do right by the soul that passed away.
Then whoever did it vanished in thin air.

CREON
Buried? *Buried?* Who'd dare to break my law?

GUARD
How would I know? It's not like they left a spade
with their name on it. The ground's so rock-hard
you can't sink a shovel or pickaxe in,
and if a cart were used it left no wheel-ruts.
Not a trace – it's like virgin soil up there.
The security guard couldn't credit it
when he took us to the corpse at sun-up.
As for us lot, we were stunned – we thought
the body had gone at first till we spied
a mound of white flesh, sprinkled with dirt,
like a new potato lying in the earth.
We poked about to see how it had got there:
had a gun-dog buried it like a bone?
But the culprit weren't no creature, that was clear,
so we began laying the blame on each other,
every man among us effing and blinding
till we were all in a rage at being accused.

There we were, going at it by the crime-scene,
when one man piped up "We have tell Creon.
Summat like this can't be kept dark." That stopped us.
We hung our heads, full of fear, knowing he was right.
So then we drew lots and – guess what, Sod's Law –
muggins here picked the short straw. Which is how come
I've come – not by choice, but from fate singling me out.
I can see you're not best pleased with me, either:
no one likes the man who fetches bad news.

CHORUS

I don't say this lightly ... I know it's odd ...
But I see a hand in this – the hand of the gods.

CREON

Save your wind to blow your porridge with.
The gods? What have they to do with it?
Why should the gods care for the corpse of a traitor?
Because he came to torch their temples,
shit on their altars, and break their laws,
they gave him a hero's send-off? The gods?
You're either senile or insane, you lot.
  I'll tell you who's behind this – those who muttered
against my law the minute I passed it,
going behind-backs and whispering in palms
and plotting my overthrow on street corners.
There are always men who'll slip you a coin
– no questions asked – for doing their dirty work.
Whoever buried that body was bribed.
  Money talks. Money corrupts. It makes the guard
unlock the gate for enemy troops
or pretend not to see the looters.
It brings foreigners here for easy pickings.
It forces young girls to open their legs
for seedy old men. It turns wife against husband,
son against father and worker against boss –
and it keeps spreading its foul disease,
like a bruised apple in a fruit bowl
passing its rottenness onto the rest.
  The men with the spades and those who paid them
are as crooked as a dog's hind leg.
I'm warning you, if you don't find them
and bring them here, death won't be good enough for you,
I'll have a rope throttling your neck till you croak
and I won't loosen the noose even when
the truth's out.

GUARD

Am I allowed to say something?

CREON

Go, go – every noise your voice makes grates on me.

GUARD

Do I grate on your ears? Or deeper inside?

CREON

What's it matter which? You just grate, that's all.

GUARD

When a man harms you, you've good cause to hate him.
But his voice – that's just a sound in the air.

CREON

It's all air with you – you talk through your arse.

GUARD

If I'm all talk, I can't have done it, can I?

CREON

Of course you can – you did it for money.

GUARD

I thought leaders were meant to have judgment.
You've judged me guilty without holding a trial.

CREON

Everything you've said *proves* you're guilty.
The only way to lodge an innocent plea
is to fetch the culprit. Do I make myself clear?
Find the man who did it and bring him here.

exit CREON

GUARD

I hope he *is* found, obviously –
but that'll be pure luck, not down to me.
Either way you'll not see me again.
I came with no hope of leaving in one piece –
but here I am still, against all odds,
with my head on my body – oh, thank you, gods!.

exit GUARD

CHORUS

Wonders never cease –

and nothing's more wonderful than man.
Only he can walk on water,
climbing waves higher than fells,
riding the whale-roads
with just a sail and planks of wood.

Through every season you see him,
behind his mule,
cutting turf and drilling seeds and turning clods,
the rain and sun beating on his head
but nothing shifting him –
he keeps the line straight to the end.

Salmon and herring snag in his nets,
cows swollen with milk graze in his croft,
wet-nosed dogs run to him
with grouse and pheasant in their mouths.
There's no creature he's not subdued:
horses carry him over hills,
bulls let him slip a ring through their nose,
whales give him their meat and blubber.

Nature may scream and sing,
but only man can speak words,
and set his thoughts down on paper,
and use those thoughts to frame laws
for his own good.

No creature is as canny –
he builds fires to warm himself,
houses to live in,
roads to travel on,
towns where he dwells among neighbours
safe from the lonely wilds.

There's only one thing he's not beaten.
And that's death.
Death – the eighth gate.
Death – the tunnel to nowhere.
Death – the window with no view.
Death – the door that slams shut
once you've passed through.
Death – which you can defer
but never defeat.
The eighth gate.

Terrors never cease,

and nothing's more terrible than death.
On his bad days,
man can be terrible, too.
When his cleverness turns to deceit,
when he abuses his gifts:
breaking the law,
thumbing a nose at the gods,
finding ways to be cruel,
inventing new weapons ...
Being human doesn't stop a man being inhuman. ...
Nor a woman.
Men and women like that aren't welcome here ...
If we find them, we'll batter their door down. ...
If we find them, we'll chuck them out of town.

Enter GUARD, with ANTIGONE

CHORUS
There's a turn-up. It's Antigone, in't it ...
But it makes no sense. Brought here by that guard. ...
I can't believe *she*'s broken Creon's law.

GUARD
She has. Why else would I have brought her here?
We caught her burying the body. Where's Creon?

CHORUS
She's her father's daughter, you can see,
proud, headstrong, high-strung as a mare ...
But it can't have been her who were there.

enter CREON

GUARD
Never say never. You got so wild with me
last time, I swore I'd never come back.
But then the fattest slab of luck in all my life:
I spotted this girl. In the act. Just like that.
No need to cast lots this time – I volunteered.
And I didn't dally on the road – I ran.
So there you go, she's all yours, just as ordered.
Now I've done my bit I'll be getting off home.

CREON
Hang on, there's been some misunderstanding.
This young woman you've brought – she's family.
The daughter of my brother-in-law, Oedipus.
My late sister's child. My *niece*, fathead.

Not only that, she's due to marry my son.

GUARD
I don't care who she is. I nabbed her
covering the corpse over, so I grabbed her.

CREON
This is no time for jokes. Do you realise
what a serious matter this is?

GUARD
It's plain as duck-eggs, in't it? I saw her
with the body. She was breaking the law.

CREON
With the body? Or burying it? Let's be clear.

GUARD
If it's the only way to get through to you,
I'll tell the whole story from start to stop.
So I leave with your threats ringing in my ears,
meet up with the other lads, and we go back
to the corpse. Our aim's to wipe the earth off
and leave it lying in the open again,
but that's no easy task because by now it's turned
squishy and mouldy, mashed up in the earth,
and bluebottles are buzzing round, and maggots
seething in the skin, and some of the cracks
are oozing pus and blood and gore and slime,
which make the soil stick to the flesh when we try
to brush it off, but at last we're done,
the yellow-grey corpse stripped bare beneath the sky,
and we move off a few feet and stop upwind
where the worst of its stench won't reach us,
but then a wind whips up, which lessens the stench
but also, as it strengthens, blows leaves and dust
and seedpods in our eyes: it's one of those flurries
you get on the tops, a wild pollen gust
axeing upwards from the valley bottom,
as though the gods were in a strop and had sent
a whirlwind, and we have to shelter for a while,
lying low among bracken and ling,
until the gale drops and we raise our heads
and there's the girl slap-bang in front of us,
so close we can hear her sobbing and crying,
she's like a hen-thrush returning to the nest
and finding it empty, a straw cradle

rocking in the wind and all her young gone,
aye, seeing the body bare of the earth-rug
she'd wrapped it in is like his death all over again,
and she curses those who've done it then sets to
filling the jug she's brought, big as a bucket:
it's earth, not oil or water, she fills it with,
but when she lifts it to the heavens
then pours the red sandy soil over three times,
it's more a birth-rite than to do with death.
  Not that we're standing idly by, just gawping:
in a blink, we've seized and trapped her like a deer.
But she doesn't fight back, and when we read her
the riot-act for trying to bury the corpse
twice over she just stares us in the face:
no denials, no excuses, nothing at all.
I feel sorry for her: such calm and courage.
Then it hits me. Joy of joys! I've slipped the rope.
It was me swinging from the gallows before
but now, if I tell Creon, it'll be her.
So I do myself a favour and bring her in –
a man's got to look after his own skin.

CREON
It's no wonder you're staring at the ground.
Is what he says true?

ANTIGONE
Yes, I admit it.

CREON *[to GUARD]*
There are no more charges against you. Go.

exit GUARD

But you ... Let's keep this brief, shall we. You knew
I'd passed a law against burying him?

ANTIGONE
Sure I did. You made enough fuss about it.

CREON
So you knowingly – wilfully – broke the law?

ANTIGONE
It depends whose law you're talking about.
This was a law passed by you, not Zeus.
Justice – true Justice – wouldn't recognise it.
Rush through any clause you like, but no law

the gods make can be amended or thrown out
on the whim of a self-appointed leader.
Their laws are ancient and immutable,
not the passing fancy of some upstart.
They began in time's dawn, before we were born.
And they're laws so inscribed in our hearts
we've never needed to write them down.
1: Don't kill your family. 2: Don't breed with them.
3: Honour your parents. 4: Bury the dead.
Was I meant to break *those* laws, and be brought
to judgment in the courtroom of the gods,
my only defence that a man – a mere man –
had made me? I'm not frightened of you.
Because you've thatch on your chest and a pair
of hard-boiled eggs in your groin doesn't make you
a god. Go on, sentence me to death: so what?
We all die anyway and soonest's best
if living on means giving in to threats.
Dying's easy, but to ignore my brother,
to let him rot like a dead goat in the open –
I couldn't do it. Fine, call me bone-headed,
you should know – Bonehead's your middle name.

CHORUS

Like father, like daughter ... One hothead breeds another ...
She's vicious as a bitch that won't be collared ...
She's wilder than a vixen in a hen-coop ...
If she dun't back down, she'll by dead by dusk.

CREON

She's only a woman and I'm used to them.
The harder they fight, the harder they fall.
It's like iron in the forge – the rods
with no give in them are those that smash
to smithereens. I've seen it with mares, too –
they'll frisk and rear, for fear of being broken
and saddled, but slip a bit in their mouth –
the smallest bit in the stable will do –
and they're yours to kick and ride for life.
What does she have to be so proud about,
where she came from? Breaking my law was bad enough,
but then she tops it by coming here to crow,
mocking us and gobbing in our faces.
You start to wonder who's the man round here.
I'm not having it. I'm leader. The man's me.
She thinks I'll let her off because her talons are

in my son and her feet half under the table.
But having ties with me and mine is no excuse.
Being family makes it worse, in fact, and must be punished
more severely. First torture, then death.
And no ordinary death: she must be stoned –
when a woman gets above herself,
that's how we put her back in her place, below.
And I don't mean just her but her sister, too.
The two of them were in on it together.
I saw Ismene just now, hysterical she was,
tearing her hair out, half off her head –
a crime can be done and dusted in secret
but then guilt will write its letters on your face.
That's if you've not already bragged to the world,
as though evil was something to be proud of.

ANTIGONE
That's that, then, is it? I'm to be killed.

CREON
You are.

ANTIGONE
Can you just get on with it, then?
It can't be worse than being stuck here with you,
though my only crime, just to remind you,
was to arrange a burial for my brother,
which meant scrabbling in the dirt with my own two hands.
These men here know I did the right thing.
They'd tell you, if they weren't such timeservers.

CREON
What they're serving is the town, the same as me.

ANTIGONE
It's not the same. When you're a leader
people smile and smarm, they suck up to you,
they've not the guts to tell you when you're wrong.

CREON
No else one in this town sees it your way.

ANTIGONE
They all do – they're just too cowed to say so.

CREON
We've not shed young blood winning a war
so a slip of a girl can break the law.

ANTIGONE
Your law, not the gods'. Who do you think you are?

CREON
I'm the voice of this town. Doesn't it bother you
to be out of tune with popular opinion?

ANTIGONE
Popularity? You? The issue is clear:
a sister should love and respect her brother.

CREON
What about your other brother, the man
he killed, the one who stayed loyal to this town?

ANTIGONE
They were born to one father and mother,
and I love them both the same.

CREON
By honouring one,
you dishonour the other. He'd be appalled.

ANTIGONE
How do you know? He's dead. You aren't his spokesman.

CREON
I know he hated traitors, just as I do.

ANTIGONE
And I know he'd want his brother remembered.

CREON
Remembered for attacking the town he grew up in,
which Eteocles died fighting to save?

ANTIGONE
The gods expect burial rites regardless.

CREON
The patriot and the traitor have different rites.

ANTIGONE
In death everyone's the same, good or bad.

CREON
Death doesn't make an enemy a friend.

ANTIGONE
You can't judge the dead. A corpse is innocent.

CREON
Even when it's guilty of treason?

ANTIGONE
That wasn't the corpse, that was the man.

CREON
But he was a bad man. He hated his brother.

ANTIGONE
Yes my brothers did hate each other,
by the end. But I loved them equally.
I can't help it. Hate's not in my nature.

CREON
You can take your loving nature down to hell.
I'll not take lessons from a girls' school.
No woman's going to lord it over my rule.

enter ISMENE

CHORUS
Here's Ismene ... She's under a cloud ...
A cloud so black it's drained the pink from her cheeks ...
Her eyes are flooding like meadows after rain ...

CREON
To think how I raised you in my own house,
never seeing you for the snake you are,
sinking your poison in while I slept,
and laying plots against me. You've not a tongue
as loud as your sister's, but it's forked the same.
Adders, the pair of you, never so sly
as when slithering towards a grave ...
Own up: you buried the body with her, didn't you?

ISMENE
She'll deny it but yes, I'm guilty, it's true.
Justice demands that I be sentenced, too.

ANTIGONE
Justice! That's not justice, it's perjury.
When I asked for your help, you turned me down.

ISMENE
I'm walking beside you now, hand in hand.

ANTIGONE
Get off. You should have given your hand before.

I've no need of fellow travellers now.

ISMENE
We're still sisters, aren't we? Don't reject me.

ANTIGONE
It was you who rejected me. You're too late now.

ISMENE
It's never too late to be a sister.

ANTIGONE
There's only one of us on trial here.

ISMENE
If you die, what's the point in me living on?

ANTIGONE
Ask your friend over there. Ask Creon.

ISMENE
What good does it do, taunting me like this?

ANTIGONE
Taunts help remind me how you let me down.

ISMENE
That was then. Now I'm offering to help.

ANTIGONE
Help yourself. Live. I don't begrudge it.

ISMENE
But why begrudge it if I choose death with you?

ANTIGONE.
You can't chop and change. You made your choice.

ISMENE
I was giving you good advice, that's all.

ANTIGONE
Your advice was to give in. I belong
to a different world – one that honours the dead.

ISMENE
My world's the same. We all have to die.

ANTIGONE
You'll not die until your time comes,

when you're old. I'm choosing to die today.

ISMENE
Let me join you. You mustn't do it on your own.

ANTIGONE
No. This is just me. Death can't be shared.
I've made the sacrifice. I'll die alone.

CREON
I reckon they're as mad as each other.
One's been driven mad in the last few hours,
and the other's been mad since she was born.

ISMENE
Even the strongest minds start to go
when all they've known is loss and disaster.

CREON
Your disaster was to partner her in crime.

ISMENE
Life without my sister isn't worth living.

CREON
Your ex-sister. Past tense. She doesn't exist.

ISMENE
She's engaged to marry Haemon, your son.
You wouldn't kill your son's future wife?

CREON
Haemon can go and plough new furrows.
There are other holes he can drill his seed into.

ISMENE
But he chose her. He loves her.

CREON
Love!
I'll not let my son wed a hag like her.

ISMENE
Haemon will hate you, if you prevent it.

CREON
No more about the sodding wedding. It's off.

CHORUS
You can't stop them.

CREON

I'll not stop them – death'll do it for me.

CHORUS

So it's decided. Antigone must die?

CREON

Yes, we all decided it, didn't we?
I'll put the pair of them on a leading rein,
and take them indoors – that's where women belong,
tied to home not galloping at will like men.
And since they're fillies, I'll rope them tight.
They might stamp and snort like stallions,
but when death approaches out of nowhere
they'll be bolting off like nervous mares.

exit ANTIGONE and ISMENE

CHORUS

Ruin's like a beck at the year's backend:
what starts as a trickle on the tops
swells with new rain
and clouts of hail,
till by the bottom it's a roaring flood.

Ruin's like a plague-mark daubed on a door.
Once a house has been cursed,
there's no shifting the stain.

If you peer through the windows
of Antigone's house,
you'll see skeletons in the chairs.
They stretch their bony hands out
to the daughters.

The crimes of the parents
seep down like a water-mark
through the kids.
Then the kids grow up and add new crimes,
which in turn seep down.

We saw it with Oedipus.
One disaster after another,
till madness ruled the house
like an axeman,
slashing off heads and hopes.

Zeus is the only rock.

He towers above us,
ageless, beyond reproach,
always on the lookout.
No man on earth can match him.

Zeus is our only hope.
To know he's in charge up there
and will be till the crack of doom
– that's consoling, inspiring,
something to respect.

I don't knock hope:
people need it to go on.
But if you expect too much
stepping out on life's road
you'll stumble into a white-hot fire.

Who was it once said
"Those whom the gods ruin
they first confuse",
so that good seems bad
and bad seems good,

and the path shining ahead
turns out a dead-end?
Knowing what's best,
telling right from wrong:
there's nothing harder.

Here comes Haemon, Creon, your surviving son.
Let's hope he fares better than his brother did.
He looks rough, though. And he can't be best pleased
to hear you're stopping him from getting wed.

enter HAEMON

CREON
Don't jump to conclusions. Let's wait and see.
Now, son, you've heard the news about your bride,
I daresay. It's come as a blow, maybe.
You've here to have a go at your old man.
You're steamed up and want to rattle your lid.
Fair enough. But I'm your father, lad.
There's a sacred tie between us.

HAEMON
There is.

I'm the only son you have now, father.
I respect that, and I agree with you,
there's no tighter bond, not even marriage.

CREON

That's all right then, son. If you weren't happy
to set aside your personal feelings to do
as I tell you, then I'd be worried for us both.
It's what every father asks for in life,
a son who'll honour and obey him.
A man who marries badly and spawns
a useless brood gets mocked and called a tosser.
And when a son ties a knot with his tongue
he can't then undo with his teeth, he's lost.
So think on: when you're taking pleasure in a woman –
her eyes, her lips, the soft sift of her flesh –
try to stand back, preserve your judgment,
don't keep your brains in your britches,
ask yourself would she be suitable,
what's her temper like, what's her family background,
is the stock she comes from weak or sound? –
you don't want some slapper for a wife
or you'll be looking over your shoulder in bed
wondering who's been in there ahead of you.
For a woman to betray her husband,
or her town – is there anything worse?
Not in my book. So forget your bit of stuff.
She's not worth it. She's not worth *you*. She's fluff.
She's sunk her fangs in your skin like an adder –
suck the sting out before the poison takes,
she can find another husband in hell.
I won't lie to you: she's under arrest
and will soon be lying under a mound.
There's no choice. If I allow a criminal
to be a lodger in my family home,
what message is that to give the town?
A bull won't get respect from the herd
unless he shows who's master. Laws are laws:
just or unjust, we have to live by them
or there'll be anarchy. The man who sees that
is your loyal subject, someone you can trust –
you know he'll stand by you when the shit's flying.
But a man who won't fall into line
is like a brick missing from the bottom
of a wall – one shove and the whole lot comes down.
I say "man" – with a woman, it's even worse.
If one of our sex defeats us, fair enough.

But to let a woman dictate – that's shameful.

CHORUS
I'm getting on in years, and maybe age
is making my mind fuzzy, but what you say
seems right enough – we'd not dispute it.

HAEMON
The power to reason comes from the gods, father.
To set out the steps of an argument
as you have, brick by brick – it's a wonderful gift.
Far be it from me to pick holes – I couldn't,
even if I wanted, though probably others
could say where you're treading on shaky ground.
  All I can do, as your only son,
is report what's being said around town –
the comments no one dares make to your face.
I've overheard the conversations,
and I can tell you, people are upset.
"Have you ever known the like?" they're saying,
"a girl sentenced to death when all she did
was scratch out a grave for her brother's body
rather than leaving him to rot on open ground.
You'd think she be given a medal for it,
not put to death" – that's the word on the street.
  I'm on your side. I know you want the best
for me, and I'm proud of your success.
Don't throw it away by kidding yourself
you're always right. Men like that, the Lord Infallibles,
who strut around thinking they've the answers,
peer inside them and you'll find they're empty husks.
Even if you are wise, there's no disgrace
in keeping your mind open and learning more.
You see it with willows by a river:
when the water's in full spate, they bow and bend,
they dip their heads in and go with the flow,
whereas stiffer trees snap or are uprooted.
It's the same with boats, too: when the wind whips up
you take in your sails or you'll capsise.
Calm yourself, mull it over and give a yard –
that's what I'm urging. I may be young
but I'm not stupid. It would be wonderful
if we *were* born infallible. But since we're not,
the wisest course is to listen to others.

CHORUS
He has a point, sir ... You'd do well to take

his advice ... Not that he can't learn from you as well.

CREON
So I'm to be told how to suck eggs, eh?
You're going to send me back to infant school
to be taught lessons by a child?

HAEMON
If they're lessons
worth learning, why not? Forget about age,
father. Concentrate on what I'm saying.

CREON
I've to honour anarchy and rebellion,
you say? And reward those who're against me?

HAEMON
I never said reward those who're against you.

CREON
Didn't you? Isn't your girl against me?
Isn't she a criminal, pure and simple?

HAEMON
You'll not find a soul in town who thinks so.

CREON
And I've to take my orders from them now?
I'm to be told what I can and can't do by geese.

HAEMON
Come on – I thought you said *I* was childish.

CREON
I'm serious. Have I to act on their say-so?
Am I running the town for them or for me?

HAEMON
If you run it just for you, that's tyranny.

CREON
When you're leader of a town, the town's yours.
You do as you see fit. You're on your own.

HAEMON
You're wrong. No leader can survive alone.
You might as well be on a desert island.

CREON
All this fussing over a dead body,

it's women's stuff.

HAEMON

No, it's common decency.

CREON *[to CHORUS]*
He's sticking up for the rights of women, see.

HAEMON
I'm sticking up for you. Are you a woman?

CREON
And now he's sunk to cracking cheap jokes.
He'll be setting the law on me next.

HAEMON
Because I'm on the side of justice and you're not.

CREON
How can that be? I'm in *charge* of justice.

HAEMON
It's not what the gods would call justice.

CREON
Mouse! And she's a cat playing with you.
She's got you where she wants you – in her paws.

HAEMON
I'm not in yours. I'd be too ashamed.

CREON
What's shaming is to hear you spout the same piss.
You're her mouthpiece. The case for the defence.

HAEMON
I'm defending myself. And you. And the gods.

CREON
The gods don't want murderers to be buried.
Rapists, traitors, madmen, tramps – it's right they lie
in unmarked graves.

HAEMON

But this is a sister
asking to bury her next of kin.

CREON
She loves that mouldering wormbag more than you.
To feel that close to a dead brother is sick.

HAEMON
It'd be sick if she didn't feel close to him.

CREON
You'll never marry her. She'll be dead first.

HAEMON
If she dies, she won't be the only one.

CREON
So you're a big man now? You think you can
threaten me?

HAEMON
It's not a threat, it's a fact.
Somebody has to talk some sense round here.

CREON
Son, the only sense you talk is nonsense.

HAEMON
If you weren't my father, I'd say you were mad.

CREON
You just parrot her – I'll not listen to your squawks.

HAEMON
What I've been saying is what I believe –
you just don't want to hear, you drown me out.

CREON
I will now. Fetch the bitch and rip her throat out
in front of the groom, so he can wed the corpse.

HAEMON
My own father ... my own father just said that.
Perhaps these men here can stand your ravings.
Your son can't. He's had it. He's getting out.
If they ask when you last saw me, this is when.
You'll never hear a word from me again.

exit HAEMON

CHORUS
He's raw with pain ... He's too young to have tough skin ...
Let's hope he dun't do summat desperate.

CREON
That's his lookout. He's trying to make me

sorry for him with his bellyaches.
But there's no chance of him saving those two snakes.

CHORUS
Are you planning to kill them both, then?

CREON
Yes! ... No, you're right, one of them's innocent.

CHORUS
But Antigone: what's the plan for her?

CREON
I'll bring her out here and have her stoned
till the ground's bloodier than a butcher's slab
and her head's a smashed eggshell runny with slime.
No, I've a better plan, I'll draw it out,
there's a place on the moor no one ever goes,
a stone outhouse, a windowless cell –
I'll have her locked up there, walled in with bricks,
but I won't let her suffocate, not quite,
and I won't starve her to death either,
I'll keep her alive – just – on morsels of bread,
so no one can say my leadership's brutal.
She can ask those gods of hers to save her.
And when they don't she'll finally listen to what I've said:
no one should place the living below the dead.

exit CREON

CHORUS
There's nothing stronger than love.
Love of a son for a father?
Love of a sister for a brother?
Love of power, money,
religion or nation?
No, stronger than those.
Love of a man for a woman.
Love of a groom for his bride.
Even if she's the bride of death.

Love doesn't sit quietly at home.
It goes where it has to.
You'll find it in a woman's cheekbones.
In the flush on her neck.
In her eyes' black pools.
Love keeps no hours but its own.
Love lives as it likes.

Love can't be stopped.
The sea's just a puddle it hops over.
It strides across mountains.
It flies through deserts.
It creeps up when you're not looking
and grabs you by the throat.
Even Zeus isn't immune.
None of the gods are.
Whoever's gripped is driven mad.

Good men turn bad with love.
Just men become unjust.
That's what we've seen –
love stirring up a son
against his father.
Because of his bride
with that look in her eye.
The flame softly burning in it.
The fire burning in him.
The coals of desire.

Everyone loses, with love.
Except love itself.
Aphrodite, mother of Eros:
she's the only winner.
She watches from her sunbed,
her floating scallop-shell.
Having a laugh.
The laugh's not on love
it's on the lovers.
The laugh's on everyone
who's fallen in love.
The laugh's on us.

enter ANTIGONE

It's nowt to laugh about.
Sadness is filling my eyes.
I can't stop – it's like a flood.
Not just pity – anger too.
Any man would feel angry.
She's off to her sepulchre.
Her moorland crypt.
Her stony tomb.

ANTIGONE
When the sun dips behind the hills,

the earth will be lost to me forever.
I'm going to my grave
instead of my marriage.
I can see my groom waiting,
dressed in black.
My wedding bed's a barrow
where the dead lie,
my bridal chamber
a bonehouse on the moor.

CHORUS
There are worse deaths.
You've kept your good name.
You can hold your head high.
And you've your health still –
you're fit!
It won't be a slow wasting away
with disease.
There'll be no violence
with a sword.
It's not death such as
the rest of us will get.
You're going of your own free will,
and when you reach the place
you'll still be breathing.

ANTIGONE
Think of Niobe
and the living death she endured
after losing all her children
through arrogance.
Just as ivy chokes a tree
till it's all ivy,
so the hills she lived in
took her over,
till her flesh turned to limestone.
Her body lay soft on the ground
as snow fell, white on white,
and the rain slowly wore her away
till only a spring was left
where her eyes had been,
a runnel of tears,
which gushes down the hillside
to this day.
Held down by stone,
worn out by tears,
that's how it'll be for me.

CHORUS
But she was one of the gods.
You're human.
All of us here are human.
You're saying your fate's like hers
to make yourself feel better
and make yourself look good.
But humans have to die.

ANTIGONE
If you have to mock me,
at least wait till I'm dead.
You're wronging a woman
who grew up here
and who loves this town as you do –
the river, the playing-fields,
the seven gates.
Your seven gates.
A living death
in a windowless cell –
even stone walls can see
how cruel that is:
why can't you?
I thought I'd friends here.
Now I see I'm a stranger
in my own town.
The living won't miss me
when I'm sent to my tomb.
There'll be nothing
to show that I once lived,
only the wind sighing
over the tarn.

CHORUS
It was you who took the risk.
You went too far.
You can't expect to break laws
and not be punished.
Of course we're sorry for you.
But what can we do?
It's not just breaking the law
you're being punished for
but the crimes of your father.

ANTIGONE
That's what makes it worse.

What he went through
I'm having to go through again –
just because I'm his.
The guilt gets handed on
like a baton in a relay race –
a race I never asked to run,
a race I was bound to lose
because my father was also my brother,
because my mother had children by her son.
What chance did I have,
with them as parents?
I can feel their hands
dragging me down.

CHORUS

You've been loyal to your family –
that's a virtue.
But maybe too loyal.
Setting family above law and order
can't be right.
No leader will put up with it.
You're too headstrong.
You don't know how to kowtow.
That's what's destroyed you.

ANTIGONE

Unwed, unheard and unloved.
I was meant to wear a bridal gown
but they've dressed me in a shroud.
My wedding bed's a slab of limestone
and the bridegroom sighing for my body
will be the wind.
I'm looking round me one last time,
hoping a friend will appear
[enter CREON, in background]
and offer me comfort,
so I won't have to die unmourned...
[SINGS] Death – the eighth gate.
Death – the tunnel to nowhere.
Death – the window with no view.
Death – the door that slams shut forever
once you've passed through.
Death – which you can defer
but never defeat.

CREON

For pity's sake, I can't stand the noise,
won't someone put her out of her misery.
I've heard mourners singing a funeral dirge
but never a corpse singing its own.
She's only wailing to put off the evil hour
or to drive us into the ground ahead of her.
I've told you – take her off to her outhouse.
It's up to her if she lives or dies there.
I'll not have her stopping in this town.

ANTIGONE

I hear them calling – mam, dad, Eteocles.
These were the hands that washed your bodies
when you died, and now you want to hold them.
I can see Polyneices waiting, too:
laying *your* body out was the death of me,
but I've no regrets – I did right to break the law.
I'd not have done it if I'd lost a child.
I'd not have done it if I'd lost a husband.
But you can find a second husband if you lose the first;
and if your baby dies, you have another.
But when your mother and father have passed on,
you've no chance of getting a new brother.
Tell me, which of the gods' laws have I broken?
If I'm wrong, and there is one, I'll soon know
about it, once I'm gone. But if it's you men
who're wrong, I hope you get the same as me.

CHORUS

There's a wild wind raging through her mouth and brain.
It's like trying to argue with a hurricane.

ANTIGONE

Haven't you lost sons and brothers in battle?
Do you never think of them lying there,
their bodies exposed to every wind that blows,
their eyes balls of melon for the crows?

CREON

Ignore her. She's only playing for time.

ANTIGONE

Oh, I know death's expecting me, up on the moor.

CREON

Don't keep him waiting, then. Off you go
to honour your family – your slag of a mum,

your murdering brother, your motherfucking dad.
I've passed the sentence. I've nothing to add.

ANTIGONE
It's not just me being destroyed,
it's my family's long roots in this town,
ripped up by a bunch of cowards and bastards.
It's no place to live, when all the men are sods
and a woman's killed for honouring the gods.

exit ANTIGONE

CHORUS
Just think – stoned to death,
not by boulders bashing your head in
but from lying in a cell,
with no cracks to let daylight through
only the stale, damp air of a tomb.

Maybe all's not lost.
Love can work miracles.
You know the tale of Danae,
locked up in a tower as a girl
so she'd never give birth ...
but then Zeus beamed himself in
as a shaft of sunlight
and next thing she was pregnant ...

That's the gods for you.
No wall will withstand them.
There's no guard strong enough.
All security's useless
when the gods step in.

She's doomed.
Unless the gods have a different plan.
Who knows?
A man can't say
what the future will be.
You just can't see.

enter TIRESIAS

CREON
Who asked you to come, Tiresias?

TIRESIAS
I'll tell you when I'm good and ready.

CREON
Haven't I always taken your advice?

TIRESIAS
You have. You'd not have won the war without me.
If you'd not sacrificed your son, as I said ...

CREON
Megareus. Yes. I owe a lot to you.

TIRESIAS
Then listen to me. You're on a knife-edge.
There's a razor at your throat. You're standing
under a boulder and it's about to drop.

CREON
You're making me nervous. What's this about?

TIRESIAS
I was bird-watching, from my usual hide,
clear skies, the world at peace, silence all around,
just a kestrel hanging in an updraft,
when suddenly, a kerfuffle, a chorus of screeches,
wings beating and claws slashing and beaks ripping,
as every bird in heaven turned on the next,
not just the sparrowhawk on the sparrow,
but starlings on martins, cormorants on wrens,
and swans jabbing at linnets with their long necks.
I was terrified. Even me, who's seen it all,
terrified. I lit a fire to the gods
but it wouldn't catch. I chucked fat on,
I stoked it with fresh rabbit and chicken legs
which hissed and spat, but even that didn't fan
the flames – there wasn't a flicker of heat there.
I'm trained to read omens – that's my business.
Those warring birds, that damp squib of a fire
both said the same: the gods have sent a plague.
And I also know the cause of it: you.
You left the corpse of Polyneices lying
in the bracken like a picnic for wild dogs.
And the birds have gorged so deep on his blood
their tongues are gummed up, and they can't sing.
It's for that the gods are paying us back.
Pride and stubborness – those are your faults, my son.
We all lose our way sometimes, but when the wise man
sees he's gone wrong he admits it and turns back,
while the stupid man keeps on and makes things worse.

Do right by the dead, Creon. Why murder a man
when he's dead already? That's my message.
It's your interests, and this town's, I've come to serve.

CREON
It's one whinger after another.
You've all got it in for me. And I know why –
money's been changing hands, blackmail's rampant,
you're trying to bribe me into burying that corpse.
Well I won't. Not even Zeus can make me.
Forget about the stench of a dead man –
it's the living who've been corrupted that stink.
I see why they call you a prophet, old son –
profit's your god, anyone can buy you off.

TIRESIAS
If you won't listen, there's no point telling you.

CREON
Telling me what? I can't follow you.
You're like a swallow twittering in the eaves.

TIRESIAS
Let me ask – do you value intelligence?

CREON
Of course. Intelligence is a gift.
Whereas stupidity ... stupidity's a plague.

TIRESIAS
A plague that's infecting you, Creon.

CREON
I'll not trade insults with a blind old bat.

TIRESIAS
Blind? When I'm the one who sees what's coming?

CREON
Blind, aye, and a liar. The only futures
you lot deal in are those that fill your coffers.

TIRESIAS
Trust a tyrant to talk of coffers.

CREON
Tyrant? I'm the leader of this town.

TIRESIAS
There'd not be a town to lead but for me.

CREON
You had your moments – till you sold yourself.

TIRESIAS
I've said enough. You won't want to hear the rest.

CREON
Go on, tell me – someone's paying you to.

TIRESIAS
You think I'd stoop that low?

CREON
No, even lower.

TIRESIAS
Here's something I'll tell you for nothing.
The gods are asking an eye for an eye,
so any day now a child of yours will die
in exchange for the children you've taken,
the one you walled up when she should be walking
freely around, and the one you left to rot
on top when he should have gone underground.
You got it wrong, twice: the one you buried
should have been left out and vice versa,
and for that the gods are after your blood,
they've let the dogs out, a rabid pack of furies
howling and slavering to tear you to bits.
Would I say all this because I've been bribed?
No, I'm saying it because I know the future.
My ears ring with the cries from your house –
not those your wife howled for Megareus
but her screams for your other son, still to come.
Not only that – I hear the boots of men
whose sons are no longer young soldiers
but corpses rotting on the battlefield,
and the wind has wafted the stench back home,
where it fills the people with hate for you,
and their boots are coming to settle the score.
And if it scares you to hear that, if your mouth's parched,
if your heart's racing, if your legs quake, tough.
When I warned you all you did was scoff.
You deserve it all. As for me, I'm off.

exit TIRESIAS

CHORUS
Such terrible things he said ... His instinct's strong,

though ... Trust me, he'll be spot-on ... In all my long
years in this town, I've never known him to be wrong.

CREON

I agree with you. That's why I'm terrified.
Confused too – I don't know what to do.
I've my pride to think of. I can't lose face.
But if holding out means ruin and disgrace ...

CHORUS

You have to act, Creon. Make the right choice.

CREON

Which is what? Tell me. I'm in your hands.

CHORUS

Free Antigone from where she's walled up.
And let her brother be buried in a grave.

CREON

You're saying cave in – that's your advice?

CHORUS

Yes, and be quick about it. When the gods step in
to punish someone, they move like lightning.

CREON

I've not got where I am by surrendering ...
But when the gods are against me ... It's soft ...
But I can't beat the gods. Right – I'll do it.

CHORUS

Do it yourself. Now. Don't leave it to others.

CREON

I'm on my way. I'll take a spade to dig
a grave for Polyneices then I'll set her free.
All that on my own. I've come round, see.
I'm doing what the gods want. I'm on their side.
So long as I live, I'll do what they decide.

exit CREON

CHORUS

He's on his way to dig a grave
then save the girl and make things right
so we can dance at the seven gates.

To the god with a thousand names.

A hundred names. Seven at least.
Seven names for our seven gates.
Dionysus.
Bacchus.
Iacchus.
Osiris.
Child of Zeus.
Son of Semele.
King of Satyrs.
Dionysus!

Mountains, seas, deserts –
they're all yours.
The theatre of Dionysus!

We see you everywhere.

In the smoke of a fire.
The steam off mulled wine.
In the green of a hillside
thick with pine.

See you and hear you.

In the song of a beck.
The silence of rock.
In the cries of women
sent mad by your cock.

Smell and touch and taste you.

In bitter green ivy.
A feather-soft nape.
In the blood-black blisters
of fresh-cut grapes.

You're everywhere.
But this town's your home.
This plague-ridden town.
Don't let it die on you.
Come quickly with your doctor's bag.
Your healing bottles.
Your home-made cures.
Your herbs and poultices.
Come down from the hills
and make us well.

Then we can live again.
Light the lanterns.
Lay out a banquet.
Buy you a drink
and get pissed together.
Take our lasses
onto the dance-floor.
Swing them round
till we're knackered.
then lie with them
in the hayfields
staring up at your stars.
Come to us, Dionysus, come!

enter MESSENGER

MESSENGER
What jokers the gods are. What a tease.
Some they give prizes to and some they ruin,
and there's no knowing why, or who it'll be.
A day since I was down and Creon was up.
I'd have given the world then, to be him.
It was Creon who put our town in order.
Led the army out. Saw our enemy off
at the seven gates. Topped every opinion poll.
Flourished in his private life too. Happily married.
With two sons who couldn't have been closer.
Now all that's gone. He's as good as dead.
He might dress the same and have his luxuries,
but underneath, inside, he'll be a corpse.
I'd not swap with him now if you paid me.
Without happiness, power means nowt.

CHORUS
By the sound of it, you've bad news for us.

MESSENGER
I have. News of a death. Which someone living
is guilty of.

CHORUS
Who's guilty? ... Who's dead?

MESSENGER
Haemon's the dead one. And the hand that killed him ...

CHORUS
Was his father's or his own?

MESSENGER

Officially, his own.
But it was anger with his father made him do it.

CHORUS
See, exactly as Tiresias said.

MESSENGER
I'm here to report. I leave analysis to you.

CHORUS
Here comes Eurydice, look, Creon's wife.
Is she passing by chance – or has she heard?

enter EURYDICE

EURYDICE
I was by my door, my hand on the latch,
when I heard you talking. The air felt hot.
I was taking flowers for Megareus,
my eldest son, some say he jumped, others
he was pushed, others again that some bargain
was struck with Tiresias. I don't know –
I don't know that I can bear to know –
but I thought if I mourned his loss and prayed
for his soul and thanked the gods for saving this town,
I'd start to feel better. I don't kid myself
the dead come back but they can live in our hearts
if our hearts are at peace and I know my son
can find a home in mine but for the picture
I have of him falling through air, the long drop
from the tower and his body in a heap,
and if a man can barter his son what stone
is he made of, what ice freezes his veins,
but I don't ask, I wasn't thinking of that,
I was only on my way to lay flowers.
So there I was, by the door, when I heard you just now.
I couldn't catch every word, only one, Haemon,
and then another word, death, next to his.
It can't be, I thought, they're confusing the names,
Haemon's my living son, I'll ask my husband,
he'll know, but he wasn't there, he'd gone.
My hand slipped from the latch, I dropped to the floor,
servants had to help me up, I walked out
in a daze through the heat-haze, but I'm here, see.
I'm used to bad news – you may as well tell me.

MESSENGER
It's true. You need to meet the facts head-on
so as to believe them – that's how grieving works.
I was there, I saw, I won't spare you the detail.
  I followed Creon up the hill, onto the moor,
where Polyneices lay, or bits of him did,
the odds and sods left by jackals and dogs.
He bundled them up in a cotton sheet,
and said prayers, and sprinkled water on,
being careful not to wet the sticks he'd laid
for a fire: with so little left to bury,
he'd settled on a cremation instead.
Once Polyneices was ash, we heaped stones
to commemorate him. Then we hurried
to where Antigone was, in her outhouse,
but before we reached it a voice reached us,
flung by the wind, a man's voice, full of despair.
Creon knew it at once. As the voice howled,
he howled at us, "Hurry, it's my son Haemon,
you're younger than me, run ahead and look,
there's a gap under the lintel, climb in
and see – if it's not his voice, I'm mad,
and if it is his voice I soon will be."
  So we ran on, and ducked under the lintel,
and though it's small, that outhouse, the far room,
the bridal cell, was high enough for Antigone
to hang herself – she'd torn strips from her dress
to make a rope and hooked them to a beam,
and there she was, still dangling, and there he was,
Haemon, howling his head off, his arms
round her waist, the bride and groom embracing.
"What are you doing, son?" Creon shouted,
when he saw. "Leave her. It's madness. Let's go."
Haemon just stood there, staring daggers at his dad,
then he spat in his face, a gob big as a toad,
and, still saying nowt, drew his sword and lunged
at him, but Creon saw the blade coming
and stepped aside. Maybe Haemon felt bad
at having gone for his old man; maybe just tired.
He looked weary and defeated any road,
and propped his sword, blade up, in front of him,
and leaned on it, stooping over like a hunchback
lower and lower till the blade was lost,
bedded in his belly, and the tip was poking
through his back. Blood pouring from his gut,
he dragged himself across to Antigone,
hugging her waist and pulling down till the rope snapped

and the two of them fell together on the floor,
his leaking blood making her cheeks bloom red,
their bodies entwined on the outhouse bed,
a wedding night like no other, the bride
feeling nothing as she lay with her legs wide,
the groom only agony – till he died.
The end of pleasure, the end of love,
and all because one man refused to budge.

exit EURYDICE. Silence. Pause.

CHORUS
What do you make of that? She went without a word.

MESSENGER
She's not the sort to make a show of feeling.
She'll mourn with friends and servants, in her house.

CHORUS
I'm worried. A grief that doesn't use words
has been known to come out in worse ways.

MESSENGER
Maybe – so passionate and yet so quiet.
I'll go after her. You could be right.

exit MESSENGER

CHORUS
Here comes Creon,
stewing in guilt,
torn apart,
all the wrongs he's done
buried to the hilt
in his son's heart.

enter CREON, with HAEMON on a stretcher

CREON
Drop your law, they said.
I didn't listen
and now he's dead.

CHORUS
To kill a son:
there's no worse thing
a father can do.

CREON
You're wrong. There is.

I killed two.

CHORUS
Two sons. Too true.
Now you know what justice is.

CREON
Justice is harsh –
the gods have been rougher with me
than I was with Antigone.
But I don't complain.

CHORUS
You deserve it.

CREON
I deserve it.
I stand here
while they stick the boot in.
I savour the pain.

Enter MESSENGER, with EURYDICE on stretcher

MESSENGER
I hope you mean that, because I've more for you.
I couldn't stop her. I got there too late.

CREON
The gods are greedier than I thought.
My sons weren't enough for them.
They had to take my wife as well.

MESSENGER
Her heart was half-broken anyway.
She'd hardly begun weeping for Megareus
when the news about Haemon came through.
She stumbled from the house to hear it
and once she'd heard she stumbled back.
I could hear her moving round the room.
She's safe, I thought, not thinking of the knife.
There she stood, the wooden handle in her heart,
a circle of red lapping out from it
like a ring of ripples in a peaty tarn.
I stepped forward to pull the blade out,
but she beat me to it. It didn't take much,
a gentle twist to cut the last threads, that's all,
then she fell, floated almost, with a smile,
till I said your name, and that I'd fetch you,
at which her look turned to hate, and she cursed you

as she lay there twitching on the floor,
cursed and cursed you till her last breath was done,
the husband who'd murdered her two sons.

CREON

To be a leader, I thought,
a man must be hard as stone.

CHORUS

Being hard isn't leadership.
You should have learned to give.

CREON

A stone has no heart.
A stone doesn't feel guilt.
Let me be stone
Let me join my wife and son.

CHORUS

When the gods want your suffering to end,
they'll tell you. Men like us can't intervene.

CREON

Let me kill myself then. I'm bad news
for the town. It's you I'm thinking of too.

CHORUS

Do what you have to. We won't stop you.

CREON

I'm going then. I'm gone. I'm no one.

exit CREON

CHORUS

The brave and the beautiful
die before their time.
So do the arrogant.
Hubris is a crime.

So be wise. Be humble.
Don't go it alone.
Or the gods will come down on you
like a ton of stone.